I0059535

Bean Counting
for Authors

Bean Counting for Authors

Christina Mercer

Bean Counting for Authors
© 2016 Christina Mercer

No part of this book may be reproduced in any form whatsoever without prior written permission of the publisher except in the case of brief passages embodied in critical reviews and articles.

Distributed in the U.S.A.

ISBN: 978-0692619971

Cover art by Chelsea Starling
Graphic art by Rachel Allen Dillon
Formatting by Novel Ninjutsu

Christina Mercer
P.O. Box 1845
Shingle Springs, CA 95682
www.christinamercer.com

IMPORTANT LEGAL DISCLAIMER

The information provided is for informational purposes only and is not intended to be official legal, accounting, or other professional advice. In accordance with IRS Circular 230 Disclosure, and to ensure compliance with requirements imposed by the U.S. Internal Revenue Service, you are hereby informed that any tax advice contained in this book is not intended or written to be used, and cannot be used, for the purpose of (i) avoiding penalties under the Internal Revenue Code or (ii) promoting, marketing, or recommending to another party any tax-related matters addressed herein.

Contents

Introduction

The term "Bean Counting" has been used playfully (*or even critically*) to describe the activities by those—namely us nerdy Accountants—who fastidiously count each and every "bean" to ensure the down-to-the-penny accuracy of financial transactions. Counting beans is not what you would call an adventurous or exciting endeavor, but it *is* an important and necessary one. And though accounting for every bean coming into and going out of your business may not have you twirling in the streets, paying less in taxes and saving beans for the future is pretty great, right? Plus, it can help you avoid a day when *not* accounting for them correctly invites our nation's Big-Bean Counters to dip their ladles into your pot!

Okay, enough about beans . . .

I am one of those weirdly ambidextrous creatures who is both an Accountant and an Author (and, yes, I am quite *literally* ambidextrous and have had the occasional interest from scholars studying such anomalies). My goal here is to bring some insight to Authors who are not also weird . . . *ahem* . . . Accountants, and who might benefit from some help on the Accounting and Taxation side of things. Blending my two worlds is exciting for me and in fact does have me twirling in the streets. And though these two professions couldn't be more different in their main functions, Authors come closer to becoming mini-Accountants than they realize. Why? Because once *anyone* becomes an official business owner, he/she crosses into the realm of, well, BUSINESS, and that includes tending to Accounting and Taxes.

Originally, I shared some of the guidance found within this book in a ten-part blog series at www.indie-visible.com. After gaining positive feedback and encouragement from fellow Authors and others in the writing industry, I compiled/polished/fluffed all ten posts, added LOADS more content, including some handy visuals, and wrapped everything up in one convenient book. Though my target audience is Authors (and Creative types), much of the information provided can be used by many other business owners. My hope is that those serious about managing their businesses will find value in what is shared, and maybe, just maybe, they will watch their "beans" sprout into a vibrant wealth of green.

Chapter One
When Being an Author
Means Business

Business versus Hobby

So, you're an Author—pre-published or published—living in the land of imaginary lands and creatures and/or playing with fun and amazing facts, doing what you love best, creating all that wonderful "right-brain-y" stuff, until you realize that being an Author also means you have to swing over to that boring, yet oh-so important logical brain where you stick on your business hat and get serious about a few things.

Namely: Income, Expenses and Taxes, *oh my!*

To start this bean-counting book off right, we need to first determine what it truly means to be a BUSINESS. Yes, a bona fide Business in the eyes of IRS *(and those eyes can be quite big and bulgy)*. So, let's get to it, shall we?

Most of you probably know that income earned from writing is taxable, even if those earnings barely pay for an ink cartridge (not uncommon when you're first starting out!). But does that income mean you are an official Business according to our mighty tax institutions? It would be nice. Businesses can claim expenses, and all those seminars, web sites, editors, designers, business cards, bookmarks, etc. add up. Sometimes, those costs are greater than the income you make.

Sometimes you incur them with *zero* earnings in a year *(mac-n-cheese, anyone?)*. So, can you still be considered a Business when your activity generates losses?

The answer: Maybe.

Being a Business owner means that you file a tax schedule known as a Schedule C-Profit or Loss From Business attached to your personal tax filing at year end.

Note: I am referring to a Sole-Proprietor business. If you formalize your business into an LLC, Partnership or S-Corporation, you will have an entirely separate tax filing versus a Schedule C. More on that topic in the next chapter!

The bottom line income/loss that you generate from your Business increases/decreases your other taxable income. Losses are common for young Businesses and also for many in the arts, and since losses reduce your tax bill there are a number of tests to pass before IRS deems your activity a LEGITIMATE BUSINESS versus what they call a HOBBY. Hobby income *MUST* be claimed *(yes, that's right!)*, but Hobby expenses (aka Hobby Losses) can *only* be taken to the limit of the income you made, and those have to go through an additional crunching formula on a different schedule you may or may not qualify to file.

Are we having fun yet?

Keep in mind that even though a Hobby doesn't give you the tax advantage of writing off all of your expenses, it's best to treat your writing this way until it becomes seriously Business-fied (*I'm an Author, so I create new words*).

An important principle to help determine if your writing is "Business-fied" is that you have a serious intent to operate your business at a profit.

Sounds pretty straight-forward. Most of us Authors want to make money over and above what we spend. So, by that definition, we are in Business, right?

The answer again: Maybe.

You *MUST* be able to *prove* your intent, and to do this the IRS has criteria—nice and complex because torturing us is their true goal. Okay, maybe not, and in actuality they do want us to strive toward a profitable Business because that means *(can you guess?)* more tax revenue.

A super general way to prove you have a Business instead of a Hobby is by showing a net profit (income minus expenses) *three out of five years.*

> **"A super general way to prove you have a business instead of a hobby is by showing a net profit (income minus expenses) three out of five years."**

In other words, Net Losses (when expenses are greater than income) more than two years out of a five-year span are *typically* a no-no. But this isn't set in marble. There are other rules in place to justify losses and retain your Business status.

Remember how I said their rules were complex? *Stay with me!*

Here is an EXAMPLE LIST I put together of "the more, the merrier" factors that could help an Author prove legitimacy as a Business:

📖 You are generating royalties (which means you are getting one or more year-end 1099s), or earning other sales revenue or income. If no income is generated yet, you have a completed manuscript that you are either shopping around or getting ready to publish on your own and have proof to show your efforts (copies of query letters, replies from agents or editors, correspondence with freelance experts helping you with tasks to self-publish).

📖 You have a web site, social media presence, etc. that showcases yourself as a writer/Author.

📖 You attend writing seminars, conferences, signings, speaking events, panels, etc.

📖 You keep a thorough and separate record of all income/expenses apart from personal stuff (business bank account, business PayPal or Square account, dedicated credit card, etc.).

📖 You have or have applied for a resale license (not required in states with no Sales or Use Tax).

📖 You have or have applied for a Federal Tax ID Number (not required unless you have employees, but can be a helpful legitimize-*r*).

📖 You advertise/promote your book(s).

📖 You spend the bulk of your work-week engaging in your business (full-time hours are ideal), and you are able to prove those hours via a log or calendar of sorts.

In addition, and more formally, the IRS has NINE factors it uses to determine a Business from a Hobby (I've added some clarification after each).

⚠️ WARNING: Eyes may glaze over. Caffeine helps!

Note: IRS does not intend for these to be exclusive, and no one factor is conclusive. Not every factor applies in every situation.

1.) The MANNER in which the taxpayer carries on the activity—In other words, you handle your business in a businesslike manner, you keep solid records, keep personal and business money separate, acquire proper licenses, hire professionals, etc.

2.) The taxpayer's EXPERTISE—This means you have extensive knowledge in your activity, which can be attained by degrees, certificates, completed workshops, self-study programs, seminar attendance, etc.

3.) Taxpayer's TIME and EFFORT—You spend a solid amount of time engaging in your business activity. Full-time is best. And proof of this is extremely helpful.

4.) Expectation that business ASSETS may appreciate in value—If you have large business assets, such as property, the appreciation may be considered in lieu of profits.

5.) Taxpayer's SUCCESS in other activities—A history of turning profits from other endeavors, especially if they relate to writing, can support that you are aiming to make this business a profitable one, too.

6.) HISTORY of income and losses—You've made profits in the past and are incurring losses because of economy or book marketplace changes out of your control.

7.) AMOUNTS of profits and losses—Showing profits three out of five years.

8.) Taxpayer's FINANCIAL STATUS—You rely on this income for support.

Note: this factor has been disputed because it's difficult to make a living as an Author right away.

9.) Elements of personal PLEASURE—If the activity is being done for fun.

Note: this factor also opens itself to scrutiny. Taking pleasure in your career does not mean that you aren't running a business aimed at making a profit.

These factors are, again, mostly used to test activities creating losses. Once you show regular profits, the question of status pretty much vanishes.

Some Authors show a regular profit flow by combining income from related activities. Examples are those writers who also design book covers, speak at events for a fee, or hire themselves out as freelance editors. Multi-tasking this way under one Business "umbrella" can be a great way to offset expenses and keep your legitimate wheels rolling.

In summary, learning the difference between a HOBBY and a BUSINESS is an important first factor for understanding how you formally treat your writing. And remember, the Hobbyist writers of today can quickly bloom into the Business owners of tomorrow.

And that brings me to one more recommendation: Keep solid records no matter what you are!

Okay, if you're a dog or a unicorn then you don't have to keep records, but I digress . . .

Get in the habit of keeping records early on and you will save yourself and any tax professionals you use down the road from pulling hair out *(yes, I've seen my share of bald spots during tax season)*. Because this is such an important element, I've dedicated an entire chapter to Keeping Books (see Chapter 3).

Chapter Two
Structure

Business Entities Compared

Ah, the question of structure—that ever important element of fiction, film, and in the realm of counting beans, business.

For many Authors and other small businesses, the most common structure choice is a SOLE PROPRIETORSHIP *(try saying that ten times!)*. Authors are typically the "sole" owners of their businesses, their transactions from an accounting standpoint are fairly simple, and their income levels (especially at the start) will often deter them from setting up more complex entities. They have the simplest tax filing method, with all business income/expenses being reported on a Schedule C-Profit or Loss From Business for a Sole Proprietor, which is an attachment to their regular tax return, as compared to other structures that require separate business tax filings/reports. They contribute and withdraw money at will, without any affect on their profits/losses, and they are not considered an employee for payroll reporting purposes. For these reasons and more, it is easy to see why the choice for many is a Sole Proprietorship.

However, as much as "common" and "simple" seem ideal, there are reasons why a different choice should be made. Some will choose to start their businesses right off the bat under a different structure. Others may come to a point when *changing* their entity structure down the road is in line.

You might wonder why any sane person would want to add more complexity with accounting, taxes, and other legal *stuff* when it comes to their business, and no sane person does without good reasons. Choosing a different entity structure can offer options and/or advantages not found with a Sole

> **"The Bottom Line: Understand all of your options so that you can choose wisely."**

Proprietorship, whether or not those occur right from the start or after being in business for awhile. Many Authors, in fact, never veer (nor ever plan to veer) from a Sole Proprietorship, and that is perfectly fine. But I would still encourage all to read on, as the information given might prove useful somewhere down the road.

The Bottom Line: Understand all of your options so that you can choose wisely.

Choosing an entity type is mainly based on one or more of these FACTORS:

- ➢ The number of owners
- ➢ Costs of setup and administration
- ➢ Personal liability
- ➢ Tax implications

There are FIVE MAIN BUSINESS STRUCTURES from which to choose: Sole Proprietorship, Partnership, C Corporation, S Corporation, and Limited Liability Company (LLC). Though similarities can exist, each entity differs in their formation, management, taxation, legal liability, and life expectancy. So, let us introduce and compare:

1.) SOLE PROPRIETORSHIP—*Why Would an Author Choose a Sole Proprietorship?* Because it is, by far, the simplest. Most Authors fit perfectly fine here and will choose otherwise *only* when another structure type is either required or offers benefits that outweigh the ease of setting up and running a Sole Proprietorship. In fact, becoming a Sole Proprietor is so easy that an Author might already be one before he/she realizes it!

EXPLAINED: As mentioned above, this is the *easiest* structure to understand, and the most common one used by Authors and small, single-owner businesses. Basically, a Sole Proprietorship is an unincorporated business with no existence or legal distinction separate and apart from its owner. No formal filing or event is required to create this business type (keep in mind that rules apply with regards to city business licenses, fictitious names, hiring employees, and reselling goods). A Sole Proprietorship ends when the owner either dies or dissolves the business by choice.

MAIN PROS: It is the simplest structure for a single owner (husband-wife can also be "as one" in a joint venture). The business tax filing is handled on a Schedule C attached to the personal tax return (no separate tax filing is required). The owner is not an employee for payroll purposes, and unless employees are hired, no Employment Identification Number is required (an owner's social security number is sufficient). The owner has total control of all management and company assets. Even though not an employee, an owner can still deduct health insurance premiums in full (special rules and handling required).

<u>MAIN CONS</u>: Owner takes on *personal liability* for all debts and activities. Once business profits hit $400 or more in a year, Self-Employment Tax kicks in at a current rate of 15.3% (this pays for Social Security and Medicare; more details about this tax in Chapter 5-Flow). When substantial profits are made, the risk of audit often rises higher than with other business structures.

2.) PARTNERSHIP—*Why Would an Author Choose a Partnership?* Partnerships allow two or more owners to join hands in business, as compared to the single-owner entity of a Sole Proprietorship. An Author could join with one or more other Authors (or others in the writing industry) to engage in activities such as publishing books, running co-founded web sites, hosting co-founded events, or combining efforts to accomplish an array of activities. If smartly done, Partnerships can accomplish synergistic outcomes greater than those achieved by individuals working on their own. Sometimes 1 + 1 = 100.

Okay, the Accountant part of me is shaking her head because 1 + 1 does not mathematically equal 100, but she does *accept that combined efforts can equate to a more profitable business.*

<u>EXPLAINED</u>: This entity is similar to a Sole Proprietorship in some respects and different in others. A Partnership is an entity that allows the presence of multiple owners, each contributing to the business capital and each sharing in the profits and losses. Two types of Partnerships exist: General and Limited. Limited Partnerships are more common in real estate ventures and/or startup companies with investor partners who do not participate in the business operations. For

the purposes of this discussion, we are referring to General Partnerships—entities where all partners are engaged in the operations of the business. Sharing is key with a General Partnership. The Partners are collectively in charge of its formation, management, taxation, and dissolution. And all this "sharing" contributes to both the pros and cons of this structure type:

MAIN PROS: A Partnership allows two or more owners to join together in a business. It spreads out costs and risks to more than one individual. Ownership and profit/loss split percentages can be set up differently from one another for optimum tax savings. Partners are not considered employees for payroll purposes. It is a "pass-through" entity, which means the Partnership itself does not pay Federal Income Tax. It combines expertise and networking contacts. It promotes mutual support.

MAIN CONS: Profits are shared. Disagreements can create problems. Partners are *jointly and individually liable* for all debts of the Partnership. A separate tax filing/informational report (Form 1065), which includes a distinct Employment Identification Number and a Balance Sheet is required. An annual minimum Franchise (state) Tax, regardless of profits, may be levied (depends on the state). Share of profits pass through to partners and are subject to Self-Employment Tax on their personal tax returns.

3.) C CORPORATION (governed under Subchapter C of the IRS code)—*Why Would an Author Choose a C Corporation?*

This one might be chosen because BIG business (and big

profits) is the goal. Owner-shareholders gain protection from personal liability for debts and losses (aka *limited liability*). There is the option to sell shares to an unlimited number and varying type of investors. C Corporations can publicly trade shares. Though a *rare* choice for most Authors, in the case of large collaborations and/or when BIG money is in play, this is an entity choice that could prove beneficial.

EXPLAINED: A C Corporation is perhaps the *least likely* choice for an Author, mostly due to its high complexity. In brief, it is an independent legal entity owned by shareholders, often a *large* number of them. Most companies with over 100 owners and all publicly held companies are C Corporations. Though some small business owners choose this route, most opt for a simpler entity structure.

MAIN PROS: C Corporations offer limited liability protection to all shareholders. There is no limitation on the number or type of shareholders (they can be individuals or entities). Multiple classes of stock can be issued. It can provide simplified ownership transfers (through sales of shares). Many fringe benefits are free of payroll taxation.

MAIN CONS: This entity is highly complex with regards to accounting, taxation, and legal formalities. It is subject to double taxation (corporate profits are reported and taxed via a separate Corporate Tax Return in addition to shareholders paying taxes on dividends from those same profits). An annual minimum Franchise (state) Tax, regardless of profits, is typically levied (depends on the state).

4.) S CORPORATION (governed under Subchapter S of the IRS code)—*Why Would an Author Choose an S Corporation?* This choice offers protection from personal liability for debts and losses (aka *limited liability*). It allows a single owner the option to sell shares to others later. Shareholders do not pay Self-Employment Tax. Authors might choose this status either as single owners or when joined with others and profits are high and/or a corporate veil is desired.

EXPLAINED: An S Corporation is an independent legal entity owned by shareholders, often a *small* number of them (maximum number allowed by law is 100). S Corporations are closely held corporations that *elect* their status (after meeting certain tests) with the IRS. To clarify, an S Corporation technically begins as a C Corporation that either immediately (at formation) or after in business awhile *elects* to become an S Corporation. Another common scenario is when a company is technically an LLC that has *elected* to be treated as an S Corporation for tax purposes (see more on LLCs below).

MAIN PROS: It offers limited liability protection to all shareholders. It allows for a single or multiple shareholders. It is a "pass-through" entity, which means the S Corporation itself does not pay Federal Income Tax. Unlike with a Partnership's pass-though status, the share of net profits passing to shareholders is only subject to Ordinary Income Tax on a shareholder's personal tax return (instead of being subject to both Ordinary Income Tax *and* Self-Employment Tax).

MAIN CONS: There are complex rules with regards to accounting, taxation, and legal formalities. There are tighter rules on the number and type of shareholders (as opposed to a

C Corporation). Shareholders operating the business are paid as employees, which means tracking and paying for all pertinent payroll taxes, and salaries *MUST* be reasonable in relation to shareholder distributions of profits *(or risk facing IRS eyeballs that may deem distributions as payroll)*. A separate tax filing/informational report, which includes a distinct Employment Identification Number and a Balance Sheet, is required. An annual minimum Franchise (state) Tax, regardless of profits, is typically levied (depending on the state).

5.) LIMITED LIABILITY COMPANY (LLC)—*Why Would an Author Choose an LLC?* This choice provides protection from personal liability for debts and losses (aka *limited liability*) no matter which entity structure is elected for tax treatment. It offers the ability to be in business as a sole owner or partnered with others. It provides the freedom to change entity classification for tax purposes. Authors might consider the extra setup and maintenance of an LLC (as compared to a Sole Proprietorship or General Partnership) worth it in order to better insulate themselves from personal liability. And when profits come rolling in big time, owners can elect entity changes for optimum tax savings.

EXPLAINED: This is a fairly new (since 1977 in the U.S.) *hybrid* entity structure allowed by state statute. Its main original purpose was to allow for Partnerships to have the limited liability feature enjoyed by Corporations while retaining the ease of pass-through tax status. Each state will have its own set of rules for an LLC, but the basic elements include the option to have a single owner (known as a member) or multiple owners (members) and the right to choose which business structure the LLC will be treated as for tax purposes.

Let me repeat that last part: the right to choose which entity structure the LLC will be treated as FOR TAX PURPOSES! *Sorry to shout, but it's an impressive feature, as it offers a unique freedom not found with other entity structures.*

To illustrate: A single-member LLC is typically classified as a Disregarded Entity *(no, it's not ignored)* and taxed like a Sole Proprietorship; a multiple-member LLC is typically classified as a Partnership and taxed with the same pass-through system Partnerships use. Member(s) can also *elect* to have Corporation (C Corporation or S Corporation) tax status instead, and file taxes according to corporation rules. There are reasons (some mentioned above in the PROS for both Corporation types) when an election would become beneficial from a tax standpoint. And no matter which tax-status entity is elected, the LLC provides limited liability to all of its members.

Note: with regards to an LLC making an election to change its classification, once an election is made, the LLC cannot elect another classification change during the 60 months after the effective date of the election (an election by a newly formed LLC that is effective on the date of formation is not considered a change for purposes of this limitation).

Though "tax-status" classifications will offer different pros and cons, some *general* pros and cons of an LLC are as follows:

MAIN PROS: The setup of an LLC is less complex than with a Corporation, yet members gain the same limited liability protection shareholders enjoy. It offers flexibility with choosing entity status for tax purposes. There is no limit on the number of members.

MAIN CONS: The setup is more complex than with a Sole Proprietorship or Partnership. An imposed minimum Franchise (state) Tax, regardless of profits, may be levied (depending on the state). There are complexities with selling/dissolving ownership interests. There are varying rules state to state. In some cases, limited liability for single-members may be disputed.

Note: a single member should take care when signing contracts to ensure that the business name—often the same name as a single member—is followed by: LLC.

As you can see, Authors have choices to consider when setting up or changing their business entity structures. Many remain Sole Proprietorships for their entire careers, while others opt either right from the start or years later to form alternate structures. I (currently) run my Author business as a Sole Proprietorship and my writer collaborative business as an LLC with Partnership tax status. Those structures work best for all concerned now, but I remain open to the possibility of changes in the future.

My mottos: Stay Informed and Be Flexible *(Yoga, anyone?).*

In closing, there is a mountain of details beyond this chapter (and book) that apply to each business entity. Such is the nature of law and taxes. But I hope the key points made will help Authors understand more about the choices available to them and how each option might best suit their needs.

Now it's time for a stretch . . .

Chapter Three
Keeping Books

And I Don't Mean Fiction

So, why must one *keep books*; why maintain organized records versus stuffing whatever might be important into a random box to be dealt with at the end of the year?

Well, it could save you from an April meltdown, a throttling by a friend or relative who's offered to help you do your taxes, an outright refusal by an overworked tax professional, or if you're lucky, an agreement by said tax professional to help you, along with a hefty bill for the hours of sorting required.

Shoe boxes, paper bags, even a giant plastic garbage bag *(yeah, talk about* Hefty*)* stuffed with wads of paper had me wanting to throttle a few people back when I worked as a Tax Accountant.

But seriously, good recordkeeping is a *MUST* for every successful business. Not only should you know how in the heck your business is doing financially *throughout* the year, Financial Statements and tax returns simply cannot be prepared *accurately* without proper records. The better the records are kept, the more likely you will avoid tangles down the road. And believe me when I say IRS tangles need a whole lot more than a spritz of oil to straighten out. Oh, and if you thought that annoyed tax preparer was costly . . . *yeah.*

Also, know this: THE BURDEN OF PROOF IS ON YOU.

It is your responsibility to prove all entries, deductions, and statements made on your tax returns. You *MUST* be able to prove your expenses to deduct them. Proper information, actual receipts, detailed transactions, bank statements, year-end tax forms such as 1099s, payroll reports and forms, sales tax reports, etc. all contribute to substantiating what you claim to be true on your tax returns. And you *MUST* have your business records available for the IRS to inspect upon request. The more complete your records are if this happens, the less hair loss will occur during their intense *comb-through*.

So, how long do you need to keep records on the chance the IRS aims their comb your way?

There are a variety of rules ranging from two years for "this thing" to seven years for "that other thing", so as a super general rule, I say keep business records for at least SEVEN YEARS. After the seven-year mark, you should be fine to shred *general stuff*.

Exceptions: Always retain records for real estate owned by your business, as those will be needed at the time of sale, and there is *no* statute of limitations in the case of fraud or tax evasion!

So, now that you know the importance of solid recordkeeping, the gist of items that help prove your income and deductions, and how long you should keep that proof handy, let's get more detailed on the *types* of records to keep and on the *methods* in which to keep them.

METHODS of recordkeeping can range from simple to complex, from manual journals and ledgers to computer-based spreadsheets or accounting software. However you decide to manage your bookkeeping is fine, as long as the system accurately shows *all* of your business transactions. And please keep in mind a couple of things: It is wisest *not* to mingle business transactions with personal ones (use separate accounts), and record things in a timely manner. Timeliness will help you avoid forgetting about or recording items in error. It will also give you a current picture of how your business is doing—to see the ups and down and trends—to help with strategy and tax planning, and help ensure that you are *actively involved* in the business side of your business. Basically, to give your important endeavor the respect it deserves.

We'll touch more on *methods* before closing, but now let's move on to the *types* of records to keep.

TYPES of records businesses should retain include anything acting as a source of transaction history. These sources often include:

- ✓ Check registers and bank statements
- ✓ Credit card statements
- ✓ Activity logs from third-party payment systems (such asPayPal or Square)

Ideally, businesses should have dedicated business accounts for all of the above, but if business and personal transactions *are* commingled, separating them out is a *MUST (highlighter pens, anyone?)*. In addition, supporting documents for business transactions should be filed in an organized way (attached directly to statements and/or filed by date or other efficient way).

Supporting documents might include:

- ✓ Purchase receipts
- ✓ Sales slips
- ✓ Deposit slips
- ✓ Paid bills
- ✓ Paid contracts
- ✓ Canceled checks
- ✓ Really, any piece of paper (digital or not) pertaining to finances that a customer, vendor, freelance professional, lender, or banker gives you
- ✓ Any contracts, insurance policies, depreciable asset papers, tax filings, payroll reports, 1099s issued, and 1099s received

And since we want things in a nice, safe, organized place, if you don't have these THREE ITEMS yet, get 'em:

1.) A good ol' file cabinet (or at least an accordion box for files and/or a binder with tabs and pocket folders)

2.) A hard drive or multiple thumb drives for backing up docs

3.) A fireproof safe in which to keep said hard drive and all extra important paper-only docs (vehicle titles, deeds, passports, etc.). Those briefcase-style fire safes work well and are cheap at around $30.

Also, because many transaction records end up in email inboxes, setting up organized email folders and moving pertinent files into those folders as they are received can aid in solid recordkeeping. EXAMPLE FOLDERS could include:

📁 Legal and Accounting
📁 Business Income & Receipts

📁 Important Correspondence (with editors, agents, publishers, freelance professionals, advisors, and promoters, either all lumped in one folder or broken down into individual folders)

Whether generated manually on columned journal/ledger sheets or derived from official accounting software, your business transactions will ultimately be used to generate what are known as FINANCIAL STATEMENTS.

⚠ WARNING: The next section is perhaps the MOST CHALLENGING material to grasp in this entire book. You have the option, of course, to skip ahead, but you've made it this far because (I'm assuming) you want to gain a better grasp on the proper way to account for your *beans*. So, let's give this whole mini-Accountant thing a whirl! However, to avoid undo head explosions, I do advise moving S..L..O..W..L..Y through this hazard zone, *er*, next section, and reread often!

Ready . . . set . . .

FINANCIAL STATEMENTS are standard Accounting reports used for a variety of business purposes, including the completion of required tax filings. You may already (even without realizing it) be creating/completing one or more of these statements in *some* format, so the following (or portions of it) may be recognizable to you. If not, this will be a great introduction to the parts and functions of the Accounting reports used by businesses in their more *formal* glory.

There are TWO STATEMENTS considered to be most important, with a third one that I will briefly introduce, as the three together complete a "full" set of Financial Statements.

PROFIT AND LOSS STATEMENT (sometimes referred to as an Income Statement) is defined as a summary of the revenues, costs and expenses for a period of time. This important Statement basically shows all income and expense items, and is the bare minimum needed to prepare an annual Schedule C-Profit or Loss From Business for a Sole Proprietor. In fact, many deductions on this Statement are transferred directly onto a Schedule C fairly easily. Here's a snapshot of a Schedule C:

SCHEDULE C **(Form 1040)** Department of the Treasury Internal Revenue Service (99)	**Profit or Loss From Business** (Sole Proprietorship) ▶ Information about Schedule C and its separate instructions is at *www.irs.gov/schedulec*. ▶ Attach to Form 1040, 1040NR, or 1041; partnerships generally must file Form 1065.	OMB No. 1545-0074 2015 Attachment Sequence No. **09**

Name of proprietor	Social security number (SSN)

A	Principal business or profession, including product or service (see instructions)	B Enter code from instructions ▶

C	Business name. If no separate business name, leave blank.	D Employer ID number (EIN), (see instr.)

E | Business address (including suite or room no.) ▶
City, town or post office, state, and ZIP code

F | Accounting method: (1) ☐ Cash (2) ☐ Accrual (3) ☐ Other (specify) ▶

G | Did you "materially participate" in the operation of this business during 2015? If "No," see instructions for limit on losses . ☐ Yes ☐ No

H | If you started or acquired this business during 2015, check here . . . . ▶ ☐

I | Did you make any payments in 2015 that would require you to file Form(s) 1099? (see instructions) . . . . . . ☐ Yes ☐ No

J | If "Yes," did you or will you file required Forms 1099? . . . . ☐ Yes ☐ No

Part I Income

1	Gross receipts or sales. See instructions for line 1 and check the box if this income was reported to you on Form W-2 and the "Statutory employee" box on that form was checked . . . . ▶ ☐	1	
2	Returns and allowances	2	
3	Subtract line 2 from line 1	3	
4	Cost of goods sold (from line 42)	4	
5	**Gross profit.** Subtract line 4 from line 3	5	
6	Other income, including federal and state gasoline or fuel tax credit or refund (see instructions) . . .	6	
7	**Gross income.** Add lines 5 and 6 . . . . ▶	7	

Part II Expenses. Enter expenses for business use of your home **only** on line 30.

8	Advertising	8			18	Office expense (see instructions)	18	
9	Car and truck expenses (see instructions).	9			19	Pension and profit-sharing plans .	19	
					20	Rent or lease (see instructions):		
10	Commissions and fees .	10			a	Vehicles, machinery, and equipment	20a	
11	Contract labor (see instructions)	11			b	Other business property . . .	20b	
12	Depletion	12			21	Repairs and maintenance . .	21	
13	Depreciation and section 179 expense deduction (not included in Part III) (see instructions).	13			22	Supplies (not included in Part III) .	22	
					23	Taxes and licenses	23	
					24	Travel, meals, and entertainment:		
14	Employee benefit programs (other than on line 19) .	14			a	Travel	24a	
15	Insurance (other than health)	15			b	Deductible meals and entertainment (see instructions)	24b	
16	Interest:				25	Utilities	25	
a	Mortgage (paid to banks, etc.)	16a			26	Wages (less employment credits) .	26	
b	Other	16b			27a	Other expenses (from line 48) . .	27a	
17	Legal and professional services	17			b	Reserved for future use . . . ▶	27b	

28	**Total expenses** before expenses for business use of home. Add lines 8 through 27a . . . . . . ▶	28	
29	Tentative profit or (loss). Subtract line 28 from line 7	29	
30	Expenses for business use of your home. Do not report these expenses elsewhere. Attach Form 8829 unless using the simplified method (see instructions). **Simplified method filers only:** enter the total square footage of: (a) your home: _____ and (b) the part of your home used for business: _____. Use the Simplified Method Worksheet in the instructions to figure the amount to enter on line 30	30	
31	**Net profit or (loss).** Subtract line 30 from line 29. • If a profit, enter on both **Form 1040, line 12** (or **Form 1040NR, line 13**) and on **Schedule SE, line 2.** (If you checked the box on line 1, see instructions). Estates and trusts, enter on **Form 1041, line 3.** • If a loss, you **must** go to line 32.	31	
32	If you have a loss, check the box that describes your investment in this activity (see instructions). • If you checked 32a, enter the loss on both **Form 1040, line 12,** (or **Form 1040NR, line 13**) and on **Schedule SE, line 2.** (If you checked the box on line 1, see the line 31 instructions). Estates and trusts, enter on **Form 1041, line 3.** • If you checked 32b, you **must** attach **Form 6198.** Your loss may be limited.	32a ☐ All investment is at risk. 32b ☐ Some investment is not at risk.

For Paperwork Reduction Act Notice, see the separate instructions.   Cat. No. 11334P   Schedule C (Form 1040) 2015

Christina Mercer

Part III   Cost of Goods Sold (see instructions)

33	Method(s) used to value closing inventory: a ☐ Cost b ☐ Lower of cost or market c ☐ Other (attach explanation)		
34	Was there any change in determining quantities, costs, or valuations between opening and closing inventory? If "Yes," attach explanation · ☐ Yes ☐ No		
35	Inventory at beginning of year. If different from last year's closing inventory, attach explanation · · ·	35	
36	Purchases less cost of items withdrawn for personal use · · · · · · ·	36	
37	Cost of labor. Do not include any amounts paid to yourself · · · · · · · · · ·	37	
38	Materials and supplies · · · · · · · · · · · · · · · · · ·	38	
39	Other costs · · · · · · · · · · · · · · · · · · ·	39	
40	Add lines 35 through 39 · · · · · · · · · · · · · · · ·	40	
41	Inventory at end of year · · · · · · · · · · · · · · · ·	41	
42	**Cost of goods sold.** Subtract line 41 from line 40. Enter the result here and on line 4 · · · ·	42	

Part IV   Information on Your Vehicle. Complete this part **only** if you are claiming car or truck expenses on line 9 and are not required to file Form 4562 for this business. See the instructions for line 13 to find out if you must file Form 4562.

43   When did you place your vehicle in service for business purposes? (month, day, year) ▶   /   /

44   Of the total number of miles you drove your vehicle during 2015, enter the number of miles you used your vehicle for:

a   Business _____ b Commuting (see instructions) _____ c Other _____

45   Was your vehicle available for personal use during off-duty hours? · · · · · · · · · · · ☐ Yes ☐ No

46   Do you (or your spouse) have another vehicle available for personal use? · · · · · · · · · ☐ Yes ☐ No

47a Do you have evidence to support your deduction? · · · · · · · · · · · · · · ☐ Yes ☐ No

b   If "Yes," is the evidence written? · ☐ Yes ☐ No

Part V   Other Expenses. List below business expenses not included on lines 8–26 or line 30.

48 **Total other expenses.** Enter here and on line 27a · · · · · · · · · · · ·	48	

Keep in mind that certain deductions are not transferred quite so directly and require adjustments according to tax law. Items involving *extra* tax considerations include inventory costing, depreciable assets, meal and entertainment expenses, gifts, auto expenses, home office, medical insurance, and sales of assets. Many of these more *complex* deductions are covered in further detail throughout this book, so do read on. But *in general*, a Profit and Loss Statement sets the foundation for the Schedule C and its accompanying forms come tax time.

Let's get into some not-so-basic ACCOUNTING BASICS . . .

To begin, allow me to introduce and explain some important terms found on a formal Profit and Loss Statement (aka Income Statement):

❖ **Sales/Revenue**—The title really speaks for itself. This is basically the total amount of all that wondrous income made from normal business activities. For Authors, *think*: royalties, direct book sales, and perhaps speaking engagement income.

❖ **Cost of Goods Sold (COGS)**—This one is a tad more complicated. It's actually computed using a formula *(don't run away!)*. For Authors, *think*: cost of books directly sold. Ready for the math? Here goes:

Beginning Inventory + Purchases (+ other direct costs)
Subtract the Ending Inventory
= Cost of Goods Sold

Before you begin rubbing those temples, let's break this down . . .

For Authors, COGS often ends up being the *cost* of printed books purchased from a publisher (typically at wholesale cost) that end up being *resold* to happy readers during the year. For those Authors who *never* directly sell any books (they let publishers handle all sales and only collect royalties) *and* they aren't selling any other goods, COGS will not pertain to their statements *(I can see some of you smiling)*. But for Authors who *are* making direct sales of books (or any other goods) at any time, this section of a Profit and Loss Statement *does* apply.

Got it so far?

Let's show *how* COGS is computed by first figuring out *each part* of the above formula in a basic <u>EXAMPLE</u>:

📕 Sally Novelist has 50 books on hand at the *beginning* of the year. She had originally paid a wholesale cost of $5 each for those books in a prior year. That means her BEGINNING INVENTORY dollar amount would equal $250 (that's 50 books multiplied by $5). As a check reference, this amount should also *match* what was recorded for the previous year's Ending Inventory.

📕 During the current year, Sally made PURCHASES of 100 books from her publisher (traditional or independent, it makes no difference) for $5 per book at a total cost of $500 (100 x $5).

📕 If Sally Novelist sold 80 of her books during the year, the current year's ENDING INVENTORY would be figured like this: 50 books on hand at the beginning of the year + 100 books purchased – 80 books sold = 70 remaining books. And since those 70 remaining books all cost her $5 each, her Ending Inventory would be $350 (70 x $5).

We can now plug the above figures into the formula to arrive at COST OF GOODS SOLD (COGS)—the cost of books *actually sold* during the year—as illustrated below:

$$\$250\ \text{Beginning Inventory} + \$500\ \text{Purchases}$$
$$\text{Subtract} \ \$350\ \text{Ending Inventory}$$
$$= \$400\ \text{Cost of Goods Sold}$$

In a case like this where the per-book cost remained constant ($5 in the example), you might be thinking that COGS could have been calculated *much* simpler by just taking the 80 books sold and multiplying them by $5. And you'd be absolutely right! If the cost of books *never* changed from purchase to purchase, that would be a fine method. But costs *do* change. Often. And that is why knowing the proper equation is a *MUST*.

Grasping this so far?

Rereading helps! Don't let equations overwhelm you. With a little patience and practice *(and multiple caffeine breaks)*, you'll soon have the hang of COGS. Take a nice deep breath and a long sip from that cup of sanity, and when you're ready, jump back in. I'm about to explain just *how* different per-book costs are handled.

When Authors pay different per-book costs from one purchase to the next (a common occurrence), those important inventory figures must be calculated using one of FOUR INVENTORY METHODS to keep track of goods. Ready to meet the Fabulous Four *(they don't bite . . . much)*?

1.) FIFO Method (First in, First out)—This method assigns the "First" or *oldest* unit cost to items sold. So, if the first 50 books Sally Novelist purchased cost $5 each, she would assign the $5 cost to the first 50 books she sold.

2.) LIFO Method (Last in, Last out)—This method assigns the "Last" or *most recent* unit cost to items sold. So, if the most recent purchase of 50 books cost $8 per book, the $8 cost would be assigned to the next 50 books sold *before* assigning a prior purchase per-book cost.

3.) Average Cost—This method assigns *(you guessed it)* an *average* cost. Basically, the *total* cost of multiple purchases is divided by the *total* number of units purchased to arrive at the per book cost.

4.) Specific Identification Method—This method uses the actual cost of *each* particular unit (more commonly used with unique/easily-segregated goods rather than a bunch of the same thing, such as books).

You can exhale now! And pat yourselves on the backs, because you now have a general understanding about the workings of Inventory and Cost of Goods Sold (COGS). This means you can fill out that pertinent section of a Profit and Loss Statement, which for Sole

Proprietors, also ends up on the upper portion of page 2 of a Schedule C, as shown below in a focused snapshot:

Schedule C (Form 1040) 2015						Page 2
Part III	**Cost of Goods Sold** (see instructions)					

33	Method(s) used to value closing inventory: a ☐ Cost b ☐ Lower of cost or market c ☐ Other (attach explanation)					
34	Was there any change in determining quantities, costs, or valuations between opening and closing inventory? If "Yes," attach explanation . . . . ☐ Yes ☐ No					
35	Inventory at beginning of year. If different from last year's closing inventory, attach explanation	35				
36	Purchases less cost of items withdrawn for personal use	36				
37	Cost of labor. Do not include any amounts paid to yourself	37				
38	Materials and supplies	38				
39	Other costs	39				
40	Add lines 35 through 39	40				
41	Inventory at end of year	41				
42	**Cost of goods sold.** Subtract line 41 from line 40. Enter the result here and on line 4	42				

I can see all those mini-Accountant hats beaming bright *(unless those are your brains on fire)*. Grab a cold drink and let us move on to the next parts of the Profit and Loss Statement.

❖ **Gross Profit**—When you take Sales/Revenue and deduct Cost of Goods Sold, you arrive at what is called Gross Profit *(hopefully not gross in any other sense)*. Gross Profit acts like a subtotal, and is simply the term used for the profit you made before deducting what are known as Operating Expenses.

❖ **Operating Expenses**—These include both generic expense categories and industry-specific expense categories. Generic expense categories are those common for many business types (advertising, insurance, office supplies, rent, etc.). Several of these categories fit nice and straight-forward in labeled boxes on the Schedule C. Industry-specific expense categories are those that are customized based on the needs of the industry or trade of a business. For Authors, these might include editing fees, conference fees, writing research, and so on (see Chapter 6-Essential Elements for a MUCH more in-depth discussion on Author expenses). Many industry-specific expenses are listed out by category under the *Other Expenses* part of the Schedule C.

❖ **Net Operating Income**—When all of the Operating Expenses are deducted from Gross Profit, we arrive at a subtotal called Net Operating Income. This marks *almost* the end of the Statement.

❖ **Other Income**—Anything else not included above will typically fall here and often pertains to income/expenses *not* directly related to normal business (Author-type) activities. Examples include: Gains and/or Losses from Asset Sales, Interest and/or Dividend Income, credit card rewards, and so on. This total amount is added to/subtracted from Net Operating Income to arrive at the ever-important . . . *drum roll, please* . . .

❖ **Net Income (Loss)**—This "bottom line" term refers to what your business made (or lost) overall for the year.

Note: some preparers deduct income taxes before arriving at a "true" Net Income (Loss), also known as Net Profit (Loss).

That's it, the Profit and Loss Statement in brief! And here's a *simple* clarifying visual for your glancing pleasure:

Basic Components of a Profit & Loss Statement	
Sales/Revenue	$8,500
COGS	1,500
Gross Profit	$7,000
Operating Expenses	1,100
Net Operating Income	$5,900
Other Income	100
Net Income	$6,000

Now that we've covered the first, fairly straight-forward Statement used by business owners, allow me to introduce you to its more complex sibling, the second Financial Statement that should be included in every *solid* set of books.

The BALANCE SHEET is the second important Financial Statement, which tracks Assets, Liabilities, and Owner's (or Shareholder's) Equity (more on those terms below). This Statement shows the "Financial Status" of a company at any given time. It is such a useful Statement that I cringe to mention this, but *(shhh!)* Sole Proprietors are not required to generate a Balance Sheet for tax filing purposes.

Note: other, more formalized business entities—Partnerships, S or C Corporations, LLCs, etc.—are required to provide Balance Sheet information.

But before you Sole Proprietors run away grinning, know that it is most prudent for *every* business owner to complete a Balance Sheet right along with the Profit and Loss Statement. Why? Tax reporting aside, the mighty Balance Sheet is used for many business needs—lenders typically require them, it acts as additional support to prove proper recordkeeping, and if you track/account for *every* monetary transaction your business makes *(which you should be doing anyway, right?)*, a Balance Sheet can be easily accomplished and will provide a clear picture of your accumulated business success. In fact, having a handle on reading and analyzing a Balance Sheet can provide a solid understanding of the current, and even future, health of any business.

Mini-lecture over. Ready for some more terms?

Generating a Balance Sheet requires what is called Double Entry Bookkeeping—at least two entries are recorded for every financial transaction in order to create what is formally known as a complete Journal Entry. Journal Entries are basically *balanced bookkeeping entries* that record *every* financial transaction a business makes. Technically, a Profit and Loss Statement *can* be prepared without any complete (in-balance) Journal Entries made, by instead using what is known as Single Entry Bookkeeping—a single entry is recorded for each transaction.

To clarify *(and help straighten some eyeballs)*, with a Single Entry system you are *basically* keeping running lists of all Sales/Revenue and all of the various Expenses, and then taking the totals of each list/category (aka "account") to make up a (formal or informal) Profit and Loss Statement. Using a Single Entry system is pretty easy—dollar amounts for transactions are listed in their pertinent categories (various income and expense "accounts") without any real accounting for how those transactions also affected bank account balances, investments, credit card debt, loans, or any other factor aside from arriving at totals to be used by Sole Proprietors filing a Schedule C.

Using the easier Single Entry system is certainly, well, *easier*. And many Authors in business use it just fine, thank you very much. But *easy* isn't necessarily the most *effective* or *efficient* or *exact* (*okay, enough "e" words*), and the goal here is to run our businesses in a professional aim-for-the-stars way, right? So, again, all businesses should be using, or striving toward using, the much-more-thorough Double Entry Bookkeeping system. And for all those planning to use Accounting Software, the Double Entry system will be a *MUST* (*yep, that's right!*), so understanding its workings ahead of time will be useful.

All good?

Let's pull those accounting hats on tighter and gain some insight on exactly how the respected Double Entry Bookkeeping system works . . .

Double Entry Bookkeeping occurs when complete (in-balance) Journal Entries are made. As mentioned, Journal Entries are recorded for every financial transaction, and each completed one will contain a "Double Entry" that ensures both of its SIDES are in *perfect balance*. This means that the dollar amount(s) on one *side* of a Journal Entry will be offset in full by the same dollar amount(s) on the other *side*.

So, what the heck are these "SIDES" I'm referring to anyway?

- ➢ The left *side* of a Journal Entry is called a DEBIT
- ➢ The right *side* of a Journal Entry is called a CREDIT

This whole SIDE-thing might be easier to grasp by further clarifying the Balance Sheet, which covers some need-to-know accounting elements.

Basically, a Balance Sheet is made up of THREE SECTIONS and TWO SIDES (yes, these *sides* are just like the *sides* mentioned above). And, again, the two *sides* are always in balance.

To illustrate, a simple equation for a Balance Sheet is as follows:

Assets =
Liabilities
+
Owner's (or Shareholder's) Equity

❖ **ASSETS**—This first *section* makes up the entire left, or DEBIT, *side* of the equation. Assets are used to operate a company. They are those items a company owns, such as Cash, Receivables, Inventory, and Equipment (aka Fixed Assets). The Asset *side* is supported (and balanced out in full) by the right, CREDIT, *side*.

❖ **LIABILITIES**—This second *section* is part of the right, or CREDIT, *side*. Liabilities are a company's financial obligations—Current and Long-Term Payables/Debts.

❖ **EQUITY**—This third *section* is the other part of the right, or CREDIT, *side*. Equity is the overall investment in a company. It's the direct monetary contributions/investments of the owner(s) (or shareholder(s)), offset by any direct withdrawals taken out by owners (or dividends paid out to shareholder(s)), and added to the company's *accumulated* Net Income (Loss) over time.

Not sure if you caught that last part . . .

Equity *includes* Net Income (Loss), which means the Profit and Loss Statement (with all those Revenues and Expenses) is *part of* a Balance Sheet. And since the section it's a part of is the Equity section, which maintains a natural right-*side* CREDIT balance, it stands to reason that Revenues (all those lovely income amounts) are treated as CREDITS (cuz they increase Equity), whereas Expenses are treated as DEBITS (cuz they decrease Equity) when making Journal Entries.

Brain swimming? Let's take a few breaths. In . . . out . . . in . . . ahhh . . .

Okay, here is a SIMPLE TRANSACTION EXAMPLE to help show how this works:

📖 Sally Novelist spent $500 for book cover design on one of her books
📖 Since the account she calls "Checking Account" is an Asset with a natural Debit balance, spending $500 from it would be a *decrease* in the form of a Credit (right-*side* entry)

Note: banks use the terms debits *and* credits *completely the opposite way! They call deposits credits and checks are called debits, so don't let that confuse you.*

🐚 Since the account she calls "Cover Design Expense" is an Expense account, and Expenses are treated as Debits, the $500 *increase* to that account would go on the left, Debit-*side* of the Journal Entry

🐚 Since the Debit and Credit *sides* are balanced perfectly by these two entries, the Journal Entry for this transaction is completed

And when you compile a *whole bunch* of Journal Entries for the year, the totals that end up in all those Revenue, Expense, Asset, Liability, and Equity accounts will make up the Profit and Loss Statement, the Balance Sheet, and really, every Accounting Report a business might need.

Absorbing this? Sort of? I know this is a DOOZY of a chapter.

For a little visual aid, take a peek at this simplified EXAMPLE:

Basic Balance Sheet	
Assets:	
Cash in Bank	$15,000
Receivables	500
Inventory (Books)	2,000
Furniture & Equipment	5,500
TOTAL ASSETS	$23,000
Liabilities & Owners Equity:	
Payables	500
Long-Term Loans	1,500
Total Liabilities	$2,000
Owners Equity	$15,000
Current Year Net Income (Loss)	6,000
Total Owners Equity	$21,000
Total Liabilities & Owners Equity	$23,000

I encourage you to revisit the above section (several times) and also explore other sources to help you get more familiarized and comfortable with the ins and outs of generating the TWO most important Financial Statements that businesses use.

All righty then, remember me mentioning I'd give a brief note about a third Financial Statement? I know, more to digest, but as promised, it will be brief!

The third, not-to-be-forgotten statement is known as the STATEMENT OF CASH FLOWS. This one is (mostly) used by businesses choosing the formal Accrual Basis (income claimed when earned; expenses claimed when incurred) versus a Cash Basis (income claimed when received; expenses claimed when paid) of accounting because it sheds light on the *actual* cash flow of a business. Since most Sole Proprietors (and some Partnerships, LLCs, and S Corporations) use a Cash Basis for their accounting purposes, a Statement of Cash Flows is, for the most part, *unnecessary*. However, it can be of service when large portions of a Balance Sheet include equipment and inventory (items always accounted for in an Accrual fashion). So, optional as it may be, it can be useful when determining the *liquidity* of a company.

And that's Financial Statements (the *hardest-core* portion of this book) in a nutshell! But before you throw a party, let's go over a bit more *(only a bit!)* on the METHODS of keeping books to help generate those important Statements.

As mentioned earlier, and especially for Authors starting out, manual ledgers/journals or do-it-yourself spreadsheets with labeled categories (accounts) for tallying up amounts can work for keeping books, but as your business grows and the transactions become numerous, a more sophisticated method will likely make things more efficient. If you also take on the task of filing your own tax returns, there are accounting software programs that work compatibly with tax software programs for ease of transferring information. I use QuickBooks for keeping books and Turbo Tax for filing taxes, and I've been generally happy with both. The programs work together, and can be used for businesses with simple recordkeeping and tax filing tasks, as well as for companies with more complex handling. Each software company has helpful guides and online resources, as do other financial software programs not mentioned here. In addition, there are many in-person training classes offered to business owners with regards to accounting basics and navigating specific bookkeeping software.

Just remember, whatever software (or do-it-yourself system) you choose, always, Always, ALWAYS seek out assistance from a professional if/when your accounting, legal, or tax needs reach beyond a *solid* scope of understanding. No matter how user-friendly software programs claim to be, there are *many* situations where adjustments and special handling are needed. Basically, if you don't understand what Statements, Forms, or Schedules are needed and/or you don't understand them well enough to fill out with minimal assistance, you really don't have a *full* understanding of how they work, and that opens doors to errors. So again, seek professional assistance if ever you are questioning the instructions/rules/laws. And please, for the love of tax-time sanity, if you use a professional, keep those *Hefty* bags at home!

Chapter Four
The Hook

Sales & Use Tax

Ah, the ever-important Hook—that thing that grabs a reader into a novel and holds them. Sales Tax *hooks* us a tad differently, and typically we don't give a lot of thought to it when we glance at a product's price tag. But that sneaky little extra hooks onto the price just the same.

Sales Tax on goods sold/re-sold (including Authored books) is imposed based on specific STATE RULES. It is considered a "pass-through" tax because the retailer is simply holding the taxes collected before turning them over to state and local taxing authorities. Authors should get clear on what is required of them regarding necessary Sales and Use Taxes imposed by those specific states in which they do business.

Let's begin by eliminating what an Author does *not* need to worry about with regards to Sales Tax collection and reporting. All book sales made through a *third-party distributor* (Amazon, B&N, etc.) are handled by the distributors themselves (this also includes having a Publisher handle their sales). The Author receives Royalty Payments rather than Sales Income, and therefore is *not* considered the retailer/one responsible for reporting sales tax. *If* this is the only way an Author sells his/her books, then Sales Tax collecting/reporting is pretty much non-existent. Nice and easy, right?

Probably . . .

Authors might still be subject to USE TAX regardless of sales, if they purchased books in a wholesale transaction (no sales tax was originally added) and then they gave away any of those books for *free* (even to themselves for personal use).

Yeah, just when you thought a zero sales price let you off the hook . . . *(see what I did there?)*

Now, for those Authors who are selling books on their own (via online order forms and mailings, out of car trunks, at signing events, or from lovely little offices), understanding Sales Tax collection and reporting is a *MUST*. This pertains to the sales of all *print* books, and in nearly *half the states*, to the direct sales of *digital* books/eBooks (be sure and check with your states on this!).

Reminder: Again, no worries when digital books/eBooks are sold through a third-party distributor who is *already* handling the collection of taxes.

Since Sales and Use Tax is state-by-state regulated, let's get to know our states a little better, shall we?

There are FIVE NO-SALES-TAX-STATES:

- ➢ Oregon
- ➢ Alaska (local taxes may apply)
- ➢ Delaware
- ➢ Montana
- ➢ New Hampshire

Yay for them! I live in California, which has the HIGHEST statewide minimum Sales Tax in the nation—currently 7.5% with certain localities adding up to 2.5% more on top of that. We have to pay for all of that golden-state sunshine. One consolation is that California happens to be a state that does not impose Sales Tax on digital books/eBooks (restrictions apply). So, yay for that!

A word on local (district) taxes: The Sales Tax rate for a specific state may be low, but local taxes can raise that rate greatly. For instance, the Sales Tax rate in Colorado is currently 2.9%, but local taxes can add up to 7.5% on top of that, making the true total tax rate in certain localities 10.4% (which even tops the golden state). And the HIGHEST current combined rate for state sales tax added to local taxes in the U.S. is . . . *drum roll* . . . a scorching 12.9% in Tuba City, Arizona.

Talk about a burn!

Note: rates mentioned above are subject to change whenever states and districts want to torture us . . . oh all right, for a variety of economic reasons. My point being, the rates I noted above may be different by the time you read this!

Okay, back to it . . .

For Authors doing business in the FORTY-SEVEN STATES that impose Sales and Use Tax *and* for those residing in No-Sales-Tax States who have NEXUS in other states (more on that below), this chapter pertains to you. To complicate things further *(oh, you knew that was coming)*, TWELVE states are known as ORIGIN-BASED when figuring out which tax rates are used, and the remaining THIRTY-FIVE states—the bulk of the nation—are known as DESTINATION-BASED. And though California is often included among the Origin-Based states, it is actually a hybrid of both—sometimes called a MODIFIED-ORIGIN state—because it is a unicorn . . . okay, because it also uses Destination-Based rules.

Eyes crossing? Allow me to clarify . . .

For reference purposes, the TWELVE ORIGIN-BASED STATES are:

- ➢ Arizona
- ➢ California (though it's really a hybrid (unicorn))
- ➢ Illinois
- ➢ Mississippi
- ➢ Missouri
- ➢ New Mexico
- ➢ Ohio
- ➢ Pennsylvania
- ➢ Tennessee
- ➢ Texas
- ➢ Utah
- ➢ Virginia

The remaining THIRTY-FIVE STATES (most of our nation) not listed in the No-Sales-Tax or Origin-Based lists are considered DESTINATION-BASED STATES.

Here's a handy map:

So, what do all those labels really mean?

Basically, businesses in Origin-Based states calculate sales tax based on the location (city/district) *from* which items are sold/shipped, and businesses in Destination-Based states calculate sales tax based on the shipping *destination* (city/district) of the goods (in an Author's case: books).

It's easier to see how these rules pertain to In-State sales—those sales made by an Author in his/her own state to a buyer residing in that same state.

EXAMPLES of IN-STATE Sales:

📖 A book shipped from one city to another city within Origin-Based Texas is taxed based on the Texas state rate plus the local/district rate of the *Origin* city from which the book was shipped.

📖 A book shipped from one city to another in the Destination-Based state New York would be taxed based on the tax rates of the *Destination* city to which the item was shipped.

📖 In the *(unicorn land)* Modified-Origin state California, sellers shipping to buyers within their same state *and* in their same city will apply their same state plus local/district rates. If they ship to other cities in CA, they will tax items using *only* the state rate. If they are officially "engaged in business" in other cities, they will tax items using the state rate *plus* the district rates of those other *(Destination)* cities.

Now, when dealing with sales to customers residing OUT OF STATE, other factors play a role in determining whether or not sales tax should be imposed. Mainly, this boils down to figuring out if sales made by businesses located in one state *also* have what is called NEXUS in other states. The same goes for businesses in No-Sales-Tax States that have NEXUS in other states that *do* impose Sales Tax. So, those businesses might not be off the *hook* completely.

All right, what the heck is NEXUS anyway and why is this term important?

When a business has a *sufficient physical presence* in a particular state through the permanent or temporary presence of *people* (employees or agents working on its behalf) or of *property* (an actual office, warehouse, or inventory housed), it has NEXUS and must abide by that state's rules regarding sales tax.

> "When a business has
> a *sufficient physical presence*
> in a particular state
> through the permanent or
> temporary presence
> of *people* or *property*,
> it has NEXUS."

You might want to read that definition one more time just to be clear . . .

SALES TAX NEXUS is fairly obvious with a business's In-State sales (a business in its home state has an obvious and *sufficient physical presence* there), but it must be *tested* for sales made in other states to determine its existence. Typically, mailing goods (such as printed books) to buyers at Out-Of-State destinations is not enough to create NEXUS in those other states. The burden often falls on the *recipients* of the goods shipped from Out-Of-State destinations to pay their home state the pertinent taxes due on goods. But "typically" and "often" do not mean "always", and since each state has varying guidelines overall with regards to *testing* NEXUS, it's best to check with a particular state to be clear on whether or not sales made/shipped there are subject to Sales and Use Tax handling by you.

Still with me? Need a caffeine refill? Go get it! I'll wait . . .

Now that you know *who* might be subject to collecting and reporting Sales and Use Tax, let's continue with *what* that means for those particular businesses (Author businesses in our case).

Acquiring a resale license from your state is a *MUST*, and most states make it fairly easy to accomplish online. Keeping a solid record of all print books purchased for resale *and* a record of the number of copies distributed from your physical inventory throughout the year(s) is another *MUST*. Records should include books sold directly to customers, books distributed directly to other retailers (such as local bookstores), and books given away for free. In other words, track *all* activity that affects your book inventory.

Note: in states requiring tax on digital book/eBook sales, you will also need to keep track of those.

Most states provide online forms to report Sales and Use Tax, and reports are typically filed annually (filing deadlines vary by state). If *large* amounts of tax are collected, the requirement can turn into quarterly or monthly reporting, so check with each state's dollar-amount threshold for that rule.

Each state will have a unique report with boxes/line items to fill out accordingly. Since I'm in CALIFORNIA, I will speak to a few of the line item amounts on that report:

❖ **GROSS SALES**—Gross Sales are determined by adding all monies you collected in exchange for your printed copies. This includes money received from individual customers *plus* money received from other retailers, such as brick-n-mortar book stores. This does *not* include any sales tax you collected.

If you sold books for a flat rate at an event and simply "included" the sales tax in the price for ease of exchange, you will need to back out the sales tax portion to arrive at Gross Sales. Here's an EXAMPLE of how to do that:

You sold a book for $10 at a local event. The pertaining sales tax rate is 7.5%. Take $10 / 1.075 = $9.30 for the Gross Sales portion.

In the case of monies earned from other retailers (such as local bookstores), use the *entire* amount they paid you as Gross Sales. Why? Because none of the amount they gave you included sales tax (or it shouldn't have). You acted as a *wholesaler* to them, and they will be the ones to ultimately collect and report sales tax on their own reports. And don't worry about this amount getting included in your total Gross Sales, either. It will end up as a *full* deduction before determining actual taxes owed (more on that below).

❖ **PURCHASES SUBJECT TO USE TAX**—Use Tax (figured using the same rates as Sales Tax) is imposed on all books you gave away for *free* and/or kept for yourself *(bummer, I know)*. Since you didn't pay the tax up front for those books, you have to pay it now. To calculate the amount for this, you'll need to figure out the per-unit cost of the books in your inventory. Take the total wholesale cost of books you purchased and divide that by the number of books you received, and then multiply this per-book cost by the number of freebies given to compute your amount of "Purchases Subject To Use Tax."

❖ **SALES TO OTHER RETAILERS FOR THE PURPOSES OF RESALE**—Remember those monies you collected and included in Gross Sales that pertained to other retailers? Well, this is where you take that same amount as a *full* deduction. <u>EXAMPLE</u>:

You gave 20 books to a local bookstore to sell on your behalf, and they sold them all during the year. They paid you a percentage of the sales price—say 60% of $10 for each book—amounting to $120 total paid to you ($6 x 20 books = $120). This amount, which should match the amount included in Gross Sales, is the "Sales to Other Retailers for the Purposes of Resale" that becomes a deduction taken before determining sales taxes owed.

❖ **SALES IN INTERSTATE OR FOREIGN COMMERCE**—These are all sales made to customers out of state and are exempt from sales tax in your own state (Remember: If you have NEXUS in other states, you'll need to abide by the rules of those states). These exempt sales are another *deduction*, washing out their inclusion in Gross Sales.

For those reporting in other states, the terms listed above may/may not vary from those found on a California report. It would, of course, be so much easier if all states acted equally with regards to Sales and Use Tax rates and reporting, but such is not the case. Another difference to note between those states imposing Sales and Use Tax is whether or not SHIPPING COSTS are taxed along with the price of an item.

In some states, if you charge for shipping as part of an order, whether or not it's listed separately from the price of the item, it's taxable. In other states, listing shipping costs separately from an item's price *exempts* it from taxation. California is one those states that does *not* tax shipping costs *if* they are listed separately. This is yet another aspect of Sales and Use Tax that will require investigation of each particular state to determine the rules.

Another question you might ask: What if during one of your reporting tax periods (whether that's a month, a quarter, or a year) your business has *zero* Sales and Use Tax due? Well, then you will be submitting zero dollars to the taxing authorities, and your report will say so. In other words, you still have to submit timely reports even when zero is owed.

Sales and Use Tax can be a tad tricky with so many state-to-state rules. Once you nail down *which* states you need to answer to, your focus can narrow to those particular requirements. And I will reiterate the importance for any business *in any state* to: Keep accurate records. The better the recordkeeping, the easier it will be to complete all of the necessary reports. This is true whether you do them yourself or farm them out to a professional. A little effort throughout the year will save you tons of time when you hit those deadlines!

Chapter Five
Flow

Profits and Business Taxes

Having good flow in a novel may seem worlds apart from having good business flow, but having the first can actually help the other. Book sales and other writer-ly income-producing activities bring money and that means things are flowing, business is good, your efforts are claiming their rewards, and so forth. A solid inflow of money is a dream come true for many Authors, but as with most profitable endeavors, taxes will claim a slice of your pie.

And now I want pie . . .

INCOME TAXES are something with which we are all pretty aware with regards to earning money. Income Taxes imposed on business profits will vary depending on the amount of profits a business generates, the type of entity structure a business falls under, and many other factors that pertain to the workings of a specific business and its owner(s). If and when Income Taxes grow to an amount that the government deems LARGE ENOUGH to be paid in *portions* throughout the year versus paid in one annual sum at tax time, ESTIMATED TAX PAYMENTS will be required. Ignoring this requirement can generate ugly penalties, so it's best to be aware of your situation and pay those estimate taxes as needed!

To explain more officially in the words of the IRS:

"Estimated tax is the method used to pay tax on income that is not subject to withholding. This includes income from self-employment, interest, dividends, alimony, rent, gains from the sale of assets, prizes and awards. You also may have to pay estimated tax if the amount of income tax being withheld from your salary, pension, or other income is not enough.

"Estimated tax is used to pay income tax and self-employment tax, as well as other taxes and amounts reported on your tax return. If you do not pay enough through withholding or estimated tax payments, you may be charged a penalty. If you do not pay enough by the due date of each payment period you may be charged a penalty even if you are due a refund when you file your tax return."

And another tidbit from them:

"If you are filing as a sole proprietor, partner, S corporation shareholder, and/or a self-employed individual, you generally have to make estimated tax payments if you expect to owe tax of $1,000 or more when you file your return.

"If you are filing as a corporation you generally have to make estimated tax payments for your corporation if you expect it to owe tax of $500 or more when you file its return."

Got all of that? Need another read-through? Go ahead, it's important.

Basically, Income Taxes are a "pay-as-you-go" tax, and once you owe $1,000 or more in Federal Income Tax ($500 for Corporations) on your annual filing, you can't get away with paying your tax bill in one annual lump sum. There are methods used to compute *how much* your Estimated Tax payments should be to avoid pesky underpayment penalties. These methods—more specifically called the Safe Harbor Rules—ensure that no penalties will apply. The general rules state that if you pay Estimated Taxes that equal at least 90% of the total tax for the *current* year OR 100% of the tax for the *previous* year (110% is required if you had an Adjusted Gross Income of over $150,000) AND you make all of your payments on or before their due dates, you will not be subject to late penalties. Again, the goal here is to make sure that your annual Federal Tax Return doesn't end up with an "amount due" of $1,000 or more.

There *are* ways to help reduce or eliminate Estimate Taxes, which include:

1.) If you happen to be an employee subject to withholding tax at your own business (if you are employed by your S-Corporation, for example) or at another business, the Income Taxes withheld on your behalf will reduce what you need to pay in for Estimated Taxes (because you are *already paying* some or all of the Income Tax imposed). In fact, you can ask your employer (who might be yourself) to *increase* your withholding amounts (via a Form W-4) as a way to reduce or possibly eliminate the need for Estimated Tax payments.

2.) You can choose to apply an Income Tax Refund you are due (if applicable) toward next year's taxes. Much like the way taxes are withheld from a paycheck and paid in on your behalf, applying a tax refund (overpayment) is an easy way to pay your taxes (or a part of them) for the next year without the obvious "pinch" to your checkbook *(yes, I know all you investor types might be frowning at the idea of giving the IRS tax-free loans via refunds. But if you're going to turn around and pay that money in a matter of months anyway, it might be worth eliminating the hassle. Or not. Your call!).*

3.) This is pretty much a given, but if you have lots of business and personal tax write-offs, your bottom-line tax will be reduced. This is yet another reminder that being informed about the potential expenses Authors can deduct is smart business.

If, after doing all you can to reduce your tax bill, you are still required to make Estimate Tax payments, the official Form used by Sole Proprietorship owners, S-Corporation shareholder-owners, partners in a Partnership, and LLC member-owners (not electing C-Corporation status) is Form 1040-ES Estimated Tax for Individuals. Payments are (typically) divided into four equal dollar amounts to cover each quarter, with payment due dates as follows: April 15, June 15, September 15, and Jan 15 of the next year. Paying online is perhaps the easiest method through EFTPS: The Electronic Federal Tax Payment System (see link on the Resources page). You can also mail your payments in with the forms.

Some important notes:

Note: if your official tax period is different than a calendar-year, different due dates will apply.

Note: Estimated Tax amounts for each quarter may not be equal due to special circumstances (the first payment is reduced or eliminated by a tax refund, you use the annualized income method, you became disabled, you retired after age 62, a casualty or disaster occurred).

Note: C-Corporations use Form 1120-W to pay Estimated Corporate Taxes.

Note: each taxing state will have their own Estimated Tax forms and rules, so check with your state's requirements!

Did you read that last note? I made sure to end it with an exclamation mark because I'm loud, *or rather*, because many states also impose State Estimated Taxes and generate penalties when State Income Taxes aren't paid in correctly just as sternly as the Feds.

All right, let us move on from Income Tax to another important business tax . . .

SELF-EMPLOYMENT TAX was mentioned briefly in the quote from IRS with regards to Estimated Taxes, and so I will reiterate it here that Self-Employment Tax *is included* when determining the proper amounts required for Estimated Tax payments. And believe me, you do *not* want to forget adding this in, as is it can rear a mighty stinger come tax time if you don't!

In brief, Self-Employment Tax is a tax imposed on Sole Proprietors, General Partners, and Members of an LLC (with Sole Proprietor or Partnership tax status) earning business profits. Since most Authors fit within one of those business structures, Self-Employment Tax is something to understand in full.

So, what exactly is Self-Employment Tax?

Self-Employment Tax is basically your contributions to Social Security and Medicare. Normally, employees of a company have those taxes withheld from their gross pay at current rates of 6.2% and 1.45% respectively. Those amounts are then *matched* by an employer, and the whole shebang (now totaling 15.3% of gross pay) is sent to the taxing authorities.

As a Self-Employed Business Owner (Sole Proprietor or Partner or LLC without Corporation tax status), you are not an employee subject to employee withholding, so instead of getting a paycheck, you get Business Profits. And these are subject to Self-Employment Tax.

> "If you earn profits of $400 or more from your business, not only should you plan for Income Taxes, you need to plan for that separate 15.3% Self-Employment."

Note: if you're an S-Corporation Owner/Shareholder who is paid as an employee, you also get/claim Business Profits, but those are not subject to Self-Employment Tax.

Remember this threshold: Profits of $400 or more from a business are subject to the total 15.3% (to pay for both the individual's withholding percentage *plus* the employer's matching percentage). This threshold amount is easily met by business owners striving for profits, and the tax percentage imposed is similar to the Federal Income Tax rate for many, so you can see why being aware of and planning for this particular tax is a *MUST*!

One other thing to remember about Self-Employment Tax is that it is added *directly* to Income Tax on a tax return (added *after* Income Tax is computed). What that means is that even if you owe *zero* Income Tax (because you had other personal tax deductions offset your business profits), you still have to pay for Self-Employment Tax. Allow me to repeat in a slightly different way: Zero Income Tax does not also mean zero Self-Employment Tax.

Bottom Line: If you earn profits of $400 or more from your business, not only should you plan for Income Taxes, you need to plan for that separate 15.3% Self-Employment Tax that too often shows up like a giant, unexpected lump on tax returns.

All of this tax planning can be daunting to think about, I know, but it's *really* important for business owners to remember that Income Tax is not the only tax imposed on a profitable business *and* Self-Employment Tax is not reduced the same way Income Tax is after applying the standard or itemized deductions, exemptions, and other "front-page" deductions on a tax return. I can't tell you how many clients of new businesses I encountered who were utterly shocked by the Self-Employment Tax they owed come tax time!

Having said all of that, a positive note is that you *do* get to take a deduction on the front page of your tax return for *half* of the Self-Employment Tax owed, and this helps reduce your overall Income Tax owed. That's something, right?

Okay, now that we've covered taxes imposed based on profits, there are TWO MORE BUSINESS TAXES worth mentioning that can play a role *regardless* of profits.

What? Taxes without profits?

Sorry, but yes . . .

If these next taxes pertain to your business, they will be owed whether you make one dollar, a million dollars, or even when your bottom line falls in the negative. Here they are:

> ➢ **PAYROLL TAXES**—If your business employs others (and/or yourself if your business is a Corporation), then you *MUST* deal with the requirements imposed by both the Federal and State Governments regarding Payroll Taxes. On a Federal level, these taxes include:

- ✓ **Federal Income Tax Withholding**
- ✓ **Social Security** (withheld and matched by employer)
- ✓ **Medicare** (withheld and matched by employer)
- ✓ **FUTA Tax** (employer paid)

Each STATE will have its own particular TAX ITEMS, too. California, for instance, has:

- ✓ **Personal Income Tax Withholding**
- ✓ **State Disability Insurance Withholding**
- ✓ **Unemployment Tax** (employer paid)
- ✓ **Employee Training Tax** (employer paid).

Because Payroll Taxation is such a giant ball of beeswax, and it requires careful recordkeeping, reporting, and on-time tax payments, I've decided to cover much more on this topic in Chapter 9-Supporting Characters. So, if you hire employees (including yourself), I highly encourage you to read more about Payroll Taxes in that later chapter.

➢ **BUSINESS PERSONAL PROPERTY TAX**—If your business owns what is referred to as "personal property" (differentiated from real property/real estate), you may also need to pay for another tax known as Business Personal Property Tax. This tax is imposed at a City or County Level, so check with your specific city/county on the rules. Basically, a (usually small) tax is figured on the *current value* of your Business Personal Property. Types of Property include *tangible* items (vehicles are excluded) such as office equipment, computers, fixtures, tools, furniture, etc. used by the business. For Authors *think*: desks, computers, copy machines, scanners, phones (any kind), filing cabinets, bookshelves, etc.

Business Property Statements are typically due on an annual basis, and all items are listed along with their values in the appropriate sections. The taxes are figured and billed to you/your business by the City/County Tax Assessor. Tax rates vary so much between cities and counties, it would impossible to list them here, but allow me to quote one California County:

"Throughout California, the property tax rate is 1% of assessed value (also applies to real property) plus any bonded indebtedness approved by the taxpayers. In Sacramento County, the average overall tax rate including bond debt averages perhaps 1.1%."

Tax Exemptions can also apply, so do check with your specific city/county to get clear on their rules. For example: Computer software (such as writing programs) and inventory for resale (such as books) are often exempt. Also, some cities (not all!) will exempt Business Personal Property owned by small, home-based businesses. Since that is a common situation for many Authors, it is an exemption worthy of checking on.

In summary, the various kinds of Business Taxes are an integral part of managing a business. Being aware of all those that pertain to your business ahead of time is extremely helpful when it comes to budgeting and ensuring that you, as a business owner, aren't blindsided by the various demands for your business pie.

And now I MUST get pie . . .

Chapter Six
Essential Elements

Common Expenses & Budgeting

Most of us know that part of running a business means paying for expenses. I mean, most businesses need "things" (tangible and intangible) to keep operations rolling. For many types of industries, there are general expenses that fall under common categories such as insurance expense, office supplies, professional fees, and so on. In addition to common costs, there are expenses that are more industry-specific, such as those typically incurred by *(you guessed it)* Authors.

But before we dive in to all of *that*, let's get clear on all of *this*:

There are rules defining what constitutes a legitimate expense in the eyes of the IRS. Here's a little explanation from our good old tax institution:

"To be deductible, a business expense must be both ordinary and necessary. An ordinary expense is one that is common and accepted in your industry. A necessary expense is one that is helpful and appropriate for your trade or business. An expense does not have to be indispensable to be considered necessary.

"Even though an expense may be ordinary and necessary, you may not be allowed to deduct the expense in the year you paid or incurred it. In some cases you may not be allowed to deduct the expense at all. Therefore, it is important to distinguish usual business expenses from expenses that include the following:
- Expenses used to figure Cost of Goods Sold
- Capital expenses
- Personal expenses

So as not to make heads spin, allow me to clarify a little on the above

THREE types of expenses that are *not deducted* in an "ordinary" fashion:

1.) Cost of Goods Sold (COGS)—As explained in Chapter 3-Keeping Books, Cost of Goods Sold is an amount computed using a formula that takes Inventory and Costs of

Sales into consideration. Because it involves a more complex computation, it isn't deducted in a straight-forward or "ordinary" way. Brief EXAMPLE to remind us about how COGS works:

If an Author purchases 500 books for resale, but only actually sells 50 in that year, he/she can only take the expense of purchasing the 50 books sold rather than the entire 500 purchased. Those 450 books still sitting in boxes are part of Inventory and are not expensed until they are sold.

2.) Capital Expenses—These are for Assets purchased that benefit the business longer than a year, such as office equipment (computer, fax machine) or furniture (desk, bookshelf). Instead of being treated like an "ordinary" deduction, Capital Expenses are depreciated over time. There are tax rules that can allow for a full deduction for an item in the year of purchase, but criteria and special handling apply (more on this topic in Chapter 7-Capitalize).

3.) Personal Expenses—These are, well, things purchased for personal use. It might be obvious why these would not be "ordinarily" expensed for a business, but gray areas do occur. For instance, a novel purchased by an Author for entertainment purposes would be considered a personal expense *(yes, reading novels helps writers in a general sense, but that really doesn't count)*. By contrast, a history book about 15th Century monarchs in England purchased by an Author writing about said monarchs fits in line with a legitimate deduction for research.

Now that we've added a bit of clarity to what defines a Business Expense, let's explore a list of INDUSTRY-SPECIFIC EXPENSES Authors might incur:

> **Advertising & Marketing (a BIG one in the world of Authors)**—paid advertising in a newsletter or on a web site; paid-for reviews (*Kirkus*, *Publisher's Weekly*, etc.); unique "swag" items, such as promotional bookmarks, postcards, buttons, pens, tote bags, charms, etc.; hiring a public relations consultant/manager; running internet ads or ads on social media, such as Facebook, Twitter, LinkedIn; blog tour fees; business cards; mailers; flyers; banners; newsletter fees; signage placed on a vehicle; prizes for a promotional raffle; business logo/branding creation fees; and I will stop here before I take up the whole page!

> **Auto Expenses**—expenses involving a vehicle (complex rules discussed in more detail in Chapter 7-Capitalize)

> **Bank Account Fees**—for designated business accounts only

> **Capital Expenses/Assets/Property**—computer equipment, fax machine, office furniture (complex rules discussed in more detail in Chapter 7-Capitalize)

> **Clothing**—themed costume for speaking/signing event, a dress for a formal speaking engagement, rain boots to research a swamp as a setting for your novel

> **Copyright Fees**

> **Cover Design**—designer fees, stock photos

> **Dues & Subscriptions**—professional society or organization dues, writer magazine subscriptions

> **Editing**—development/content editing, line editing, copyediting, proofreading

➢ **Employees & Payroll Expenses** (complex rules discussed in more detail in Chapter 9-Supporting Characters)

➢ **Events**—convention fees, vendor booth costs

➢ **Formatting Expenses**—print and/or digital formatting costs

➢ **Gifts**—to publishers, agents, clients, advertisers (strict limits apply—currently, IRS allows a $25 gift per person, per year, and recipient must have a direct relationship to your business)

➢ **Home Office Deduction** (complex rules discussed in more detail in Chapter 8-Body & Setting)

➢ **Legal & Professional Fees**—lawyers, accountants, bookkeepers, business advisors, notaries

➢ **Liability Insurance**

➢ **Licenses**—city business license, fictitious name license

➢ **Meals**—typically 50% of the cost of legitimate business meals for travel and/or business meetings can be expensed (complex rules discussed in more detail in Chapter 7-Capitalize)

➢ **Medical Insurance** (complex rules discussed in more detail in Chapter 8-Body & Setting)

➢ **Merchant Fees**—credit card processing fees from bank, PayPal, Square

➢ **Office Supplies**—pens, paper, envelopes, ink cartridges, adding machine, file folders, erasers, paperclips, stapler, thumb drives, mouse pad

➢ **Post Office Box Fee**

➢ **Postage & Shipping Costs**

➢ **Printing & Copying Costs**

➢ **Professional Development**—seminar fees, workshop fees, continuing education courses, webinars, textbooks

➤ **Rent**—office space or inventory storage space

➤ **Research Materials**—topic-specific (what you are writing about) books, other reference materials

➤ **Software**—Word, Scrivener, anti-virus program, accounting program

➤ **Stock Photos**—for web site/blog

➤ **Taxes**—business personal property tax (discussed in more detail in Chapter 5-Flow)

➤ **Telephone & Internet**—designated land line, cell phone, fax line, internet service

➤ **Trailer Design**—book trailer design fees (could also go under Advertising)

➤ **Travel**—airfare, lodging, bellman, cab fare, bus/subway fare, parking, tolls, necessary laundering

➤ **Utilities**—if renting office space (see also Home Office Deduction)

➤ **Voice Over Costs**—audio book voice over, video creation voice over

➤ **Website**—development costs, hosting fees, costs for Plugins

Not all of the items listed will pertain to every Author, and there are items not included in this list that an Author might require, but hopefully this offers an overview of the variety of specific expenses Authors *can* incur! And be sure to take note of the more complex expenses mentioned and the chapters in which they are described in more detail.

Now that we know the types of costs an Author might incur, how does he/she pay for it all?

BUDGETING is something all new and seasoned business owners alike should carefully undertake. Ideally, a budget with expenses remaining below income, while also allowing for desired profits, is the goal. This can be achieved by *working down* from estimated income and calculating how much in expenses a business can afford *or* by *working up* from estimated expenses to figure out how much minimum income is needed.

Budgets typically take the prior year(s) as a starting point for planning, but in the case of a first year in business, a budget will have to be created from scratch. New businesses will also likely require up-front capital, sometimes a significant amount, by its owner(s) to get things rolling, and so the first year (or more) is likely to generate losses. Keep in mind that this is *perfectly normal* in the beginning. Most of the time, it really does "take money to make money" and all that jazz. However, all starting capital and first year(s) of probable losses aside, making profits is the truest sign of a viable business, which is why having a budgetary plan in place is so important.

No matter how Authors are published (traditionally or independently), they will likely incur common *indirect* expenses, such as costs to run their offices (computers, hard drives, pens, paper, software, hired assistants, etc.), to support their overhead (monthly bank fees, insurance, telephone, rent, licensing, taxes, etc.), to build and maintain their social media platforms and web sites, to continue professional development (workshops, classes, books on writing craft), and to handle any other general or routine business needs that arise. Many of these types of expenses are fairly easy to budget for, as they tend to be predictable, fixed, and/or similar from year to year.

Budgeting for items that are *not* routine, for expenses *directly* related to producing books, and for costs that *differ* based on how Authors are published is a tad trickier. These can change from year to year, differ from book to book, and vary depending on the publishing paths chosen.

In fact, let's take a peek at the variety of AUTHORS, based on the PATHS taken:

📖 Authors who are purely traditionally published
📖 Authors who are purely independently published
📖 Authors who are published both ways (aka hybrid Authors)

And the above can be NARROWED FURTHER:

📖 Authors traditionally-published through large publishing houses
📖 Authors published through small presses
📖 Authors acting as their own publishers
📖 Authors who pay publishers (aka vanity presses) to publish their books for them

When considering all of the many variations of Authors, it's easy to see how budgets can differ within this profession. And all of those variations add to *other* variables, such as publishing industry changes, economic climate, and other financial influences that can modify an Author's budget.

Whew!

Before we let ourselves get too dizzy on the roller coaster of changeable times, let's bring our focus to what an Author's business is really about—creating and publishing books—and explore what this means budget-wise.

Now, you might think that Authors who are traditionally-published enjoy having an outside publisher pay for *all* of the costs that go into producing and publishing their books, which would mean they really don't need to bother with *all* of this budget business beyond a few items, and *all* is roses and sunshine.

I love roses and sunshine, and I'm not saying that they don't happen, but . . .

Even though traditional publishers *do* pay for many (or perhaps *all*) of the costs involved in getting a book published, it's important to remember that whatever those costs add up to, the publisher will seek recompense through book sales in which they take a cut (a percentage of royalties). This "cut" isn't technically an expense on an Author's budget sheet, but it *does* affect the amount of revenue an Author actually receives. Revenues will be reduced further for Authors who also have literary agents taking their cuts. Therefore, budgeting for certain expense line items may not be necessary, but budgeting for an amount of revenue (royalties) that an Author can actually count on *after* those cuts are taken is a *MUST*.

Quite often, the royalties Authors receive from traditional publishers will be in the form of royalty advances (*yes, they still happen and some are very generous*). A royalty advance is just as its name suggests—an advance payment on future royalties earned. An Author might get a nice royalty advance up front, but all royalties the Author earns in sales will go to the publisher until the advance is paid in full. Sometimes this happens quickly. Sometimes it takes years. And in some cases, an advance is never paid in full, and the Author sees nothing beyond that initial payment, though that may be just fine with an Author still rolling in a pile of up-front money. Just remember that a certain pile of money might need to sustain expenses for several years to follow.

Traditional publishers will also vary on the budgets they allow for marketing and promotional expenses. Some publishers remain quite rosy with publicity budgets, while others place stiff limits on how much is spent for a particular book. This puts many traditionally-published Authors in a similar boat as independently-published Authors with regards to budgeting for promotion— often the GREATEST expense category in an Author's world (and in many other entrepreneurs'). In fact, most

> **"Every dollar spent on advertising/marketing should generate sales over and above that dollar."**

successful businesses of *any* kind handle marketing and promotion with tremendous thought and planning, including a variety of calculations to figure out those "ideal" marketing budgets.

But rather than go on about financial formulas, the bottom line to remember for most Authors in business is that *every* dollar spent on advertising/marketing should generate sales over and above that dollar. Granted, it can take time for those initial dollars to work, but *ultimately* they should reap greater rewards, or else they're simply washing down the drain. For this reason, a solid marketing plan should include *tracking results* and making changes based on those results in a timely manner. You can make up your own logs or spreadsheets for this purpose after gathering data from each distribution site or use online services to track the data for you. Either way, giving attention to this particularly important area of budgeting can make a huge difference in your bottom line.

Okay, let's direct ourselves now to some of those *direct* costs incurred in the production of books. These costs will surely vary with each title and circumstance, but the first one (a BIG one) is certain: All Authors, no matter how they are published (how they ultimately pay for this cost) will need professional editors. Any manuscript worth its weight goes through some type of developmental/content editing in addition to line editing, copyediting, and proofing. Seasoned Authors working with editors at publishing houses will most likely "pay" for the necessary editing costs as part of their royalty advances and/or cuts. New Authors working toward submitting manuscripts to agents/publishers *and* all Authors working toward independent publishing will need to budget for editing costs as a necessary expense for producing books.

I repeat: *a necessary expense.*

Why? Because no matter how much you love your stories or how awesome you are at grammar, you still need solid editing from a different set of (expert) eyeballs.

In addition to several forms of editing, there are other necessary direct costs incurred to publish a book. Again, most traditional publishers will pay for these up front, all independently-published Authors will manage these costs on their own, and Authors who pay *(quite handsomely for many)* a third party (aka vanity press) will have them handle the tasks and costs on their behalf.

OTHER DIRECT PUBLISHING COSTS include:

- ➢ Formatting for both digital and print copies
- ➢ Book cover art and typography
- ➢ ISBN numbers
- ➢ Copyright fees
- ➢ Distributor setup fees
- ➢ Proof copies
- ➢ Shipping costs
- ➢ And more . . .

From a budgeting perspective, it is imperative for those Authors acting as their own publishers to get a clear idea of what tasks they must delegate/hire out and the estimated cost of doing so ahead of time (more on actual costs below). If, by chance, Authors happen to *also* be experts in certain areas, such as formatting or creating cover art, they can save money by providing that service for themselves.

But allow me to emphasize: *if Authors are experts!*

> **"Cutting certain corners will end up costing more in the long run."**

Taking on all of the costs up front can seem daunting to one starting out, but keep in mind that not only are these costs a hopeful investment, but paying for everything does *not* have to mean spending outside your means. This section is about budgeting, after all. What it does mean is that cutting *certain* corners will end up costing more in the long run. Poor or no editing, amateur book covers, and sketchy formatting can ruin those ever-important first impressions given to readers, ultimately inhibiting future sales, and in the long-run costing *more* time and *more* money to make things right later. It's better to be patient, save up needed funds, search out proven experts who charge a fair price, and hire them accordingly. Ensuring quality without breaking your bank is what this is really all about.

It is true that the burden for independently-published Authors to take on the full scope of publishing requires careful thought and planning, and some might wonder what the upside is to it. Though Authors acting as their own publishers do handle *all* of the management and incur *all* of the costs, they also keep *all* of the royalty shares that publishers and agents take, they have *total control* over the appearance and content of their final products, and they retain *all* rights to distribute their books however they see fit. *All* nice perks, right?

Then again, independent publishing may or may not yield the same or more sales volume or actual overall income as books backed by a publishing house (especially a "big house"). Personally, I know Authors whose books do very well with independent publishing. I also know Authors whose books do very well with traditional publishing. I know Authors who've switched camps to find better success, and I know others who struggle to make sales no matter which way they publish. A book's success really all depends . . .

It would be nice to give you a definitive answer as to which publishing path is the *better* choice, but there isn't one. Each Author should carefully weigh the pros and cons of the different options available to determine what is ultimately best for him/her.

Though varying paths are the way of it in an Author's world, and many factors play a role in each book's success, one thing *can* be controlled and is, perhaps, the greatest way to help ensure long-term sales and readership loyalty. Books that sing out QUALITY have the best chance for overall success. Once you become known for putting out a quality product, readers will trust that your next book (and the next one after that) holds to a high standard, word will spread, and success will likely follow. This *also* means that there will actually be next books to follow the first one. Though a single book *can* reap plenty of kudos and sales on its own, multiple books tend to provide a stronger presence in the eyes of readers and a more continual stream of income for Authors.

> **"Books that sing out quality have the best chance for overall success."**

Quality publishing always begins with a well-crafted and polished manuscript in place. From there, other skilled tasks are necessary before it's released to the world. The overall cost to publish a book varies, but there are *ranges* of current-day direct PUBLISHING COSTS that we can easily explore.

Note: dollar amounts mentioned are not *set in stone, costs go up and down for various reasons, and the figures are simply what I've seen firsthand in our current times. In other words, they are changeable. Also, these figures are based on fees charged by independent freelancers (not employees of publishing houses).*

❖ **Editing Costs**—Editing costs will vary depending on the type of editing services. Developmental/content editing is typically the priciest because of the in-depth critiquing of the story itself. Costs for this will range between $1,000 and $5,000 for a novel manuscript of approximately 75,000 words. Copyediting tends to be around half the cost of developmental editing, as its function is mainly to fix grammar, punctuation, and make small changes to the text. Proofreading is about half the cost of copyediting, as it takes an almost-perfected manuscript and searches out remaining typos, formatting errors, and/or errors the copyeditor missed. Using all of these estimates, an Author could plan to pay anywhere between $1,750 and $8,750 to cover all three editing services.

A broad range, I know . . .

Keep in mind that paying on the higher end does *not* automatically mean better editing. Your best bet is to get referrals, talk to other Authors who have books out that show quality editing, and base your choices on those *proven* skills. Since affordability is an important factor, editing costs may require saving for a time, coming up with creative negotiations with editors, utilizing combination packages (using the same editor for multiple editing services), and/or resorting to piecemeal scenarios (doling out a manuscript in portions). Keep reminding yourself that no matter what the cost, hiring the *right* people for your business/books is always worth it!

❖ **Cover Art**—This is another direct expense with a broad range in costs that change from artist to artist and from pre-formatted covers with basic typography to highly complex illustrations/photography and sophisticated font styles. The same guidance fits here as with finding the right editors: Referrals and a history of success are best, in addition to seeing an artist's work yourself and admiring it. Do-it-yourself cover art is one of the *biggest* mistakes independently-published Authors (who are not also expert artists) make, because nothing screams AMATEUR more quickly than a bad cover. Conversely, an amazing cover will generate that perfect eye-catching, enticing pull on readers that have them curious for more.

Paying the highest price, again, does not necessarily mean you get the best cover art, though more money is *typically* charged for more complex and/or elaborate design work. Covers can range from $300-$500 for fairly simple, yet professional designs, or cost upwards of $1,000 or more when unique illustrations or photo shoots are required. The first task is to find an artist you love, then make necessary negotiations, and then budget accordingly (which might include saving for a time).

❖ **Formatting**—The last direct expense worth mentioning here is formatting for both print and digital copies, as well as for audiobook format, if that is desired. Print and digital formatting costs will range according to the size of the book, how many types of file formats are needed (Epub, Mobi, PDF, etc.), and any special interior designs created. It can be well worth a few extra bucks to have the interior design include a bit of artistic flare. My designer used lovely vines around the chapter headings in *Arrow of the Mist* and honey bees throughout *Honey Queen* as fun enhancements.

Print formatting can cost between $200-$400, and digital formatting typically falls in the $50-$200 range. Combination/package deals can apply when getting both types of formatting, and having multiple formats certainly offers the greatest options for readers.

Audiobook formatting is really not "formatting" per se, but it does offer readers an extra *(super fun!)* format of your books. The cost of hiring a voiceover professional (aka narrator) can be $0 up front with a royalty split arrangement or anywhere from $200-$2,000 *(big range, I know)* up front with a zero royalty spit. Other variations of the above can also be negotiated between an Author and narrator. Considerations that can affect total cost are the size of the book, dialects involved (if any), sound enhancements (if any), and the popularity of the narrator you hire. Basically, if you hire a high profile/celebrity narrator *(luckeee)* they will likely cost more.

Tallying the above DIRECT COSTS for a single book brings us to a range that falls anywhere between $2,500 and $12,000 total, and even those *super broad* parameters are flexible. Smart planning includes figuring out and budgeting for the many cost variations that run from fairly simple to elaborate depending on the needs of each Author and each book being published. In addition, being familiar with those common/routine/indirect business costs that pertain to an Author's business is an important step in *overall* budgeting for a prosperous future.

But wait . . . I'm not done yet!

I'd like to mention one other important (often missed) aspect of budgeting: TIME. Budgeting our time is perhaps as vital as budgeting our dollars, and some might argue time is *more* precious because once it's lost it can't ever be recovered. Being mindful of the finite number of (work) hours in a day and using them wisely can improve the success of any business.

Some SUGGESTIONS:

✓ Utilize a detailed calendar and set certain hours and/or days aside for working your craft (plotting, writing, re-writing)

✓ Set aside time for managing the business side of things (office, legal, and accounting tasks)

✓ Set aside time for nurturing important business relationships (networking and marketing)

✓ Allow windows of time to handle any other *important* needs that arise

✓ Recognize where useless time traps may be draining valuable hours from your business and put boundaries in place

✓ Finally, understand that respecting your time in a focused and manageable way is another practice to help guide your business toward greener pastures!

Okay, now I'm done . . . Ready to get Complex?

Chapter Seven
Capitalize

Complex Expenses Part One

In the last chapter we listed Common Expenses an Author might incur. Some of the expenses were what I consider COMPLEX, and so I've dedicated two whole chapters to dig inside some of the *layers* those expenses contain. For Part One, we will explore these expenses in particular: CAPITAL EXPENSES; AUTO EXPENSES; TRAVEL, MEAL AND ENTERTAINMENT EXPENSES.

To begin, there are certain items an Author purchases that require Capitalization . . . *and I don't just mean giving them a big letter.*

CAPITAL EXPENSES are those derived from the purchase of Fixed Assets, which require special handling on a tax return. Rather than expensing the full amount of the cost, as you would an ordinary expense, the amount must be depreciated.

Allow me to quote the IRS:

"Depreciation is an income tax deduction that allows a taxpayer to recover the cost or other basis of certain property. It is an annual allowance for the wear and tear, deterioration, or obsolescence of the property.

"Most types of tangible property (except, land), such as buildings, machinery, vehicles, furniture, and equipment are depreciable. Likewise, certain intangible property, such as patents, copyrights, and computer software is depreciable.

"In order for a taxpayer to be allowed a depreciation deduction for a property, the property must meet all the following requirements:
• The taxpayer must own the property. Taxpayers may also depreciate any capital improvements for property the taxpayer leases.
• A taxpayer must use the property in business or in an income-producing activity. If a taxpayer uses a property for business and for personal purposes, the taxpayer can only deduct depreciation based only on the business use of that property.
• The property must have a determinable useful life of more than one year.

"Depreciation begins when a taxpayer places property in service for use in a trade or business or for the production of income. The property ceases to be depreciable when the taxpayer has fully recovered the property's cost or other basis or when the taxpayer retires it from service, whichever happens first."

IRS always gives us lots to digest, but basically the cost of property must undergo extra handling to arrive at the specific dollar amount expensed in a particular year. Generally speaking, depreciation is the cost of property spread over time. This is determined by each item's Class and Recovery Period, and there are (of course) numerous Classes and Recovery Periods, but Authors will *typically* acquire 5-year property, such as computers and peripheral equipment, and 7-year property, such as office furniture. Depreciation methods vary, too, using a variety of formulas. In addition *(and this is good)*, there are special rules that allow a business owner to write off larger portions, or even 100%, of the cost of property in the year of purchase. If certain criteria are met, taking Bonus Depreciation or a Section 179 Deduction can yield those types of results.

Whatever the depreciation method or special deductions taken, all depreciation reporting is handled using Form 4562. For Sole Proprietors, the total amount computed will be carried over to the Schedule C in the *Depreciation and section 179 expense deduction* box.

Still with me?

Time to uncross those eyes and dive into a few other Complex Expenses. The next few sort of go together, in that they are all about Authors on the move!

AUTO EXPENSE (*Car and Truck Expense* on a Schedule C) is our first one. Many Authors use their private vehicles for both personal and business needs, while some have purely business-owned-and-dedicated vehicles. Either way, there are TWO METHODS available to determine the amount taken for Auto Expense:

1.) Actual Expense Method—This method allows for expensing *actual* costs such as: gas, oil, insurance, registration fees, repairs, tires, washing, roadside service, and depreciation. If the vehicle is used for business *and* personal purposes, all expenses must be split between business and personal use. Business use is basically determined by figuring out the ratio of business miles driven for the year.

EXAMPLE:

Sally drove her Corolla a total of 15,000 miles for the year. 6,000 of those miles were driven specifically for her Author business. 6,000 divided by 15,000 = .40 or 40%. Her business deduction would be 40% of the actual costs.

2.) Standard Mileage Rate—This is an *optional* method that business owners can elect to use instead. Auto Expense is computed via a mileage rate set by the government. If elected, the Standard Mileage Rate is used instead of taking any actual expenses incurred. For 2015, the Standard Mileage Rate is set at 57.5 cents per mile.

EXAMPLE:

Sally's Auto Expense would be computed by multiplying the 6,000 business miles by the 57.5 cents/per mile rate to determine her total expense.

There are RULES/LIMITATIONS to be aware of when choosing the best Auto Expense method for your business, such as:

➡ If you want to use the Standard Mileage Rate, you *must* choose it in the *first* year that the vehicle is available for use in your business. You can elect to use the Actual Expense Method in later years, but you are *not* allowed to take Actual Expense in the first year and then switch to the Standard Mileage Rate in a later year. Also, if the election is made to use Standard Mileage Rate on a leased vehicle, then that method can't ever be switched in later years.

➡ It is important to log your mileage, especially if you are electing to use the Standard Mileage Rate or when your vehicle is used for both business and personal use. A log book or mileage "app" is a great way to keep track of dates, miles driven, destinations, reasons for trips, etc.

➥ Parking fees and tolls incurred by a business can be expensed regardless of the method used. Also, loan interest on a vehicle can be taken regardless of the method (based on the proper percentage of business use, of course).

➥ The Standard Mileage Rate is *not* allowed for motorcycles/scooters, or for businesses using five or more vehicles.

Vrroom!

Moving on to TRAVEL and MEAL EXPENSES . . .

These two categories are both expensed under *Travel, meals, and entertainment* found on a Schedule C, but they are also split up into TWO subcategories/boxes. One is labeled *Travel*; the other is labeled *Deducible meals and entertainment*. Quite commonly, these costs occur at the same time, as many Meal Expenses arise while traveling, though this is *not always* the case.

The best policy for *any* expenses that fall into these subcategories is to keep *actual* receipts (not just credit card or bank statements) with all pertinent information (dates, dollar amounts, reason for meetings, etc.) and *only* expense costs incurred for legitimate business purposes/business gain. The easiest method is to jot down facts right on receipts, so if and when you are ever questioned, you will have all the necessary details handy to prove those costs were directly related to business.

For Authors, TRAVEL EXPENSE could arise for costs occurring *Out-Of-Town*, such as:

- ✈ Conventions
- ✈ Workshops
- ✈ Speaking or teaching engagements
- ✈ Book signings and/or readings
- ✈ Meetings with agents, publishers, distributors, business partners, etc.
- ✈ Official club meetings
- ✈ Promotional tours
- ✈ Any other *Out-Of-Town* travel required for the needs or enhancement of the business

SPECIFIC TRAVEL COSTS might include:

- ✈ Airfare
- ✈ Baggage fees
- ✈ Car rentals, hotel valet, cab fares, bus fares, parking, and tolls
- ✈ Lodging, bellmen
- ✈ Hotel internet
- ✈ Necessary laundering
- ✈ Currency exchange fees

Did you notice I used *Out-Of-Town* when mentioning Travel Expense? Because Travel means, well, TRAVELING, which is *not* the same as toodling fifty miles away (even if that means going out of your specific town) to meet with your editor and returning to your office in time for the evening news. Travel Expenses are incurred when you travel *far enough away* from the general area or vicinity of your "tax home" (place of business) that an ordinary day's work is "substantially lengthened" and your trip "requires rest" before returning.

A few more CAUTIONARY TIDBITS:

! If you travel with a spouse who is not also an official employee, partner, or officer of your business, you cannot deduct any expenses for him/her.

! Any travel used for both recreational and business purposes will need to be analyzed for what is and is not deductible.

! Any travel outside of the USA will include further scrutiny, especially with regards to travel lasting more than one week.

Basically, the best thing to remember is that if *any* of your travel includes time and money spent for reasons other than legitimate business purposes, be very, Very aware that deduction limitations apply!

MEAL EXPENSES often occur during business Travel, but some are incurred on a local level and are perfectly legitimate deductions as long as they are (again) directly related to business. Meal Expenses show up on the Schedule C in the subcategory labeled *Deducible meals and entertainment* and are either 100% deductible or 50% deductible, depending on their purpose.

Let us explore the TWO TYPES . . .

Meals that are 100% expensed are less common (mostly having to do with employees) and some bookkeepers will lump *all* business-related meals in the 50% category for ease of recordkeeping and/or to eliminate the risk of categorizing 100% Meal Expenses incorrectly. Knowing the rules will help business owners take the proper amount of deductions on a tax return and ensure they are getting the best tax advantages available.

Here are a few EXAMPLES OF 100% DEDUCTIBLE MEALS:

🍽 The costs of food and beverages provided to employees in the form of staff-room snacks

🍽 The costs of catering an occasional employer-hosted party, such as an annual holiday party

🍽 The costs incurred from hosting an event made available to the public for advertising or promotional purposes. For instance, Authors promoting themselves at public signings can fully expense those bowls of Gummy Unicorns or cups of fruit-fizz offered to attendees.

MEALS that are 50% DEDUCTIBLE are pretty much all other business-related meals, and specific EXAMPLES for Authors might include:

🍽 Meals purchased while conducting business meetings with partners, agents, publishers, clients, investors, freelance professionals, etc.

🍽 Meals purchased while traveling on business, as mentioned in the Travel section above

With all Meal Expenses, again, be prepared to prove how those meals were *directly related* to your business. Best rule of thumb with Meals and Travel Expenses overall is to remain conservative. Overusing these types of deductions can raise flags, which is also why keeping solid records and informative receipts is a *MUST*.

Okay, so what about that "entertainment" portion of the *Deductible meals and entertainment* subcategory? Did you notice that?

Yes, businesses *can* take deductions for ENTERTAINMENT EXPENSES. *Hooray, right?*

JUST BE WARNED! These costs *MUST* be incurred for business purposes, and if there is anything that points to lavish, unreasonable, or unsubstantiated, or if costs are for activities that scream PERSONAL PLEASURE, you could invite some very not-so-entertaining scrutiny from the IRS.

Most legitimate-business Entertainment Expenses are treated the same as the 50% Meal deductions, so only half of the actual costs are tax deductible. One exception is for Entertainment costs incurred to attend an organized charitable event benefitting a registered non-profit charity. These costs can be deducted in full. But, again, no matter what percentage these costs can be deducted at, it is important to understand that *all* Entertainment Expenses must meet the rules/tests to help prove that the entertainment's *main purpose* is truly for business.

EXAMPLE: Did you attend the baseball game with your publisher to actively conduct business during the game? Did you have a general expectation of getting income or some other specific business benefit from the meeting? Did you purchase the tickets at face value or pay extra through a broker? Only face value cost is allowed.

Lots to consider . . .

As an alternative to taking an Entertainment Expense deduction for something like baseball tickets, a business can "gift" the tickets instead.

Current GIFT EXPENSE rules allow for a $25 deduction per gift, per person in a single year for business purposes. So, if the ticket cost you $30 it would be better to give it as a gift and deduct the $25 maximum-allowed amount versus deducting 50% of the cost for a $15 Entertainment Expense deduction. A Gift deduction would not require that you attend the baseball game either, and as long as the Gift is given to a bona fide business-related person. Food gift baskets work the same way. Treating these as Gifts rather than 50% deductible Meals might be the more beneficial way to handle such costs.

Before I close this section, I'll toss out a few EXPENSES that would NEVER BE ELIGIBLE for any of the above *Travel, meals, and entertainment* deductions:

⊗   Dinner with your publisher that had no business purpose or discussion

⊗   Country club dues

⊗   Athletic club dues

⊗   A concert where the noise and crowd make it impossible to conduct business

⊗   Costs of taking your spouse ice skating, even if you talked about how much money you made this month

⊗   A month-long trip to Europe for mostly personal purposes

⊗   . . . and so on . . .

As you can see, there are many complexities layering this chapter's expense categories. Understanding the ins and outs of Capital Expenses; Auto Expenses; Travel, Meals, and Entertainment will help business owners, including Authors, be better prepared throughout the year and especially come tax time.

Chapter Eight
Body and Setting

Complex Expenses Part Two

Welcome to Part Two of Complex Expenses, where I'll be digging deeper into two more important Expense Categories. The Author part of me likes to refer to these next ones as Body & Setting, but the Accountant side will give you their more formal names: SELF-EMPLOYED HEALTH INSURANCE DEDUCTION and HOME OFFICE DEDUCTION.

The SELF-EMPLOYED HEALTH INSURANCE DEDUCTION is considered a "Personal Deduction" for the Self-Employed. Why? Because the deduction does *not* show as a regular business expense on a Schedule C, and for Partnerships and S-Corporations, additional steps are required in its handling (more on that below). In a nutshell, Self-Employed Health Insurance is described by the IRS as:

> "Medical, dental or long-term care insurance premiums that self-employed people pay for themselves, their spouse and their dependents."

In order to take this deduction, there are a number of CRITERIA to be met (*cuz there is always criteria*):

✓ An individual must show either a Net Profit on a Schedule C (Sole-Proprietor), earnings as a Partner on a K-1, or wages on a W-2 as a more than 2% Shareholder of an S-Corporation

✓ The policy must be in the individual's name or the name of the company

✓ For Partners, premiums paid by the Partnership must show as income on the K-1

✓ For more than 2% Shareholders, premiums paid by the S-Corporation must show as wages on the W-2

You will notice that premiums paid by Partnerships and S-Corporations are shown as income and wages respectively. That is because (in most cases) the Partnerships and S-Corporations are also taking the premiums as a business expense. It can be a tad confusing to think about how your business takes the premiums as an expense, the amount gets added to your personal income, and then you take it as a Personal Deduction on your tax return, but such is the realm of Ping-Pong, *or rather*, taxation. What is *most* important to note, however, is that (eventually) all of those insurance premiums paid during the year will ultimately show up as a nice deduction for business owners.

Just how nice is it? Perhaps the BIGGEST reason the Self-Employed Health Insurance Deduction is so *special* is how differently it's treated as compared to a regular personal deduction for medical insurance. Allow me to clarify:

Generally, taxpayers who are *eligible* to file a Schedule A for Itemized Deductions (which means they have enough qualifying deductions to be *more* than the Standard Deduction set by the Feds) can include their legitimate medical expenses on that Schedule . . . *sort of.* The total amount of those expenses must go through a formula to determine the *actual* amount, if any, that gets counted as a qualifying Itemized Deduction. So, a taxpayer must first have enough deductions to be eligible to file a Schedule A, and then their actual medical expenses must be crunched into an amount often far below (or even zero) what the actual expenses were. *Not very special.*

By contrast, the Self-Employed Health Insurance Deduction gets the royal treatment in the land of Personal Tax Deductions because, Because, BECAUSE it sits in its full glory in a box right on the FRONT PAGE of a 1040.

Am I the only one hearing the trumpets?

Why is this wonderful? you ask. Who is this crazed Author-Accountant anyway?

The fact that the deduction sits on the front page as an "above-the-line deduction" means that you get to take it *regardless* of eligibility to file a Schedule A, and the amount is deducted from income *before* arriving at your Adjusted Gross Income (AGI). Having a lower AGI can help you avoid phase-out rules for beneficial tax breaks and is an important number used to determine taxable income, which means *less* Income Tax.

Now, do you hear trumpets?

There are, however, A FEW possible RAIN CLOUDS on this wonderfulness (*darn*):

☂ As mentioned in the criteria above, your Sole-Proprietorship, Partnership, or LLC (treated as Sole Proprietorship or Partnership) must show a Net Profit (computed *after* a deduction for half of the Self-Employment Tax and any contributions to qualified retirement plans) that is equal to or greater than the Self-Employed Health Insurance Deduction in order to claim it in full. If your business showed a Net Loss, well, then *no* deduction. If it shows *some* profit, the Deduction can be taken only up to that amount. As a small consolation, any amounts not taken for the Self-Employed Health Insurance Deduction can still be crunched over on the Schedule A (if you are eligible, of course).

☂ Eligibility for the Deduction is determined month-by-month, which means for *any months* you or your spouse were also eligible to participate in an Employer-Subsidized Health Plan, you *cannot* include the insurance premium costs for those months. In other words, this Deduction is for Self-Employed individuals who are footing the bill for their health insurance without anyone else offering to help.

☂ With regards to Qualified Long Term Care Premiums, there are coverage rules and specific dollar limits for the deduction based on a person's age. For 2015, IRS set the age and dollar limits at: Age up through 40=$380; Age 41-50=$710; Age 51-60=$1,430; Age 61-70=$3,800; Age 71 or older=$4,750

All rain clouds aside, the Self-Employed Health Deduction is pretty awesome in the world of business and taxation, and wasn't always available in its current glory. Take advantage of its benefits if you can!

Let us now explore our "Setting" . . .

The HOME OFFICE DEDUCTION can be taken if you used part of your home (rented or owned) for business purposes. Many work-at-home Authors do not realize that this deduction is available to them and that it can help reduce their tax bill.

There are TWO basic REQUIREMENTS with regards to the space used that *MUST* be met:

1.) REGULAR AND EXCLUSIVE USE—This means regular use of an exclusive area of your home, such as a dedicated office space.

2.) PRINCIPAL PLACE OF BUSINESS—This means it is the principal space where you conduct your business (you *may* be able to take a deduction if you *also* conduct business outside of the home *if* you use the space regularly, exclusively, and substantially for the business).

Once you establish that you do, in fact, use a qualified space in your home, there are TWO METHODS available to determine your deduction amount:

1.) REGULAR METHOD—This method was the required method up until 2013. Now, it is one of two methods available. The Regular Method takes the ACTUAL expenses of a home office for the deduction. This is done by calculating the business portion of the home expenses, such as mortgage interest, insurance, real estate taxes, depreciation, rent, utilities, repairs, trash collection, etc. The business portion can be figured by taking the square footage of the business space divided by the total square footage of the house, and then multiplying that percentage by the total home expenses. If the home office was not in use for the *entire* year (often the case in the first year of business), the percentage of time will further the calculation (the percentage of time would be the number of months the home office was in use divided by 12).

EXAMPLES:

◆ Rick used 250 square feet of his rented 1,250 square foot home for business purposes 9 months out of the year. The calculation of his Home Office Deduction would resemble something like this: 250 square feet/1,250 square feet = 20% business-use portion of the home. The 20% is multiplied by the annual cost of rent, renter's insurance, and utilities of $10,800 to equal $2,160. Since Rick did not use the office a full 12 months, the $2,160 is then multiplied by 75% (9 months/12 months) to arrive at a total Home Office Deduction of $1,620.

◆ Molly used 400 square feet of her owned 2,500 square foot home for business purposes the entire year. The calculation of her Home Office Deduction would resemble something like this: 400 square feet/2,500 square feet = 16% is the business-use portion of the home. The 16% is multiplied by the annual mortgage interest, real estate taxes, homeowner insurance, maintenance, utilities, and applicable depreciation for the year, which in her case totals $15,000, to arrive at a total Home Office Deduction of $2,400.

Note: applicable depreciation on an owned-home is figured using another "complex" formula.

2.) SIMPLIFIED (SAFE-HARBOR) METHOD—As its name implies, this method is far *simpler* than the Regular Method. No actual expenses play a role in figuring out the deduction, but rather a straight-forward calculation that takes the square footage of the business space—up to 300 Square Feet—and multiplies it by $5, yielding a potential total deduction of $1,500 per year. Though the Regular Method may yield a larger deduction, Simplified is, again, *simple*. There are also a couple of other BENEFITS if offers to consider:

❖ For those eligible to file a Schedule A, the allowable home-related Itemized Deductions (mortgage interest, real estate taxes) can be claimed on that form *regardless* of any Home Office Deduction taken under the Simplified Method. By contrast, the Regular Method dictates that *only* the amounts *unused* by the Home Office Deduction can be claimed on the Schedule A.

❖ Since no Home Depreciation is taken using the Simplified Method, there will not be any later Recapture of Depreciation when the home sells.

Note: as mentioned, depreciation is its own complex animal with many more layers than I can squeeze in here.

Regardless of the Home Office Deduction method chosen, if you show zero income for the year in your business, you may *not* claim a deduction. You may also *only* claim a deduction *up to* the amount of Net Profit. In other words, this deduction cannot create a Net Loss for your business. If you use the Regular Method, you may be able to carry over the disallowed expenses to the following year. Carryover rules do *not* apply for the Simplified (Safe-Harbor) Method.

Keeping good records is another *MUST*. For the Regular Method, recordkeeping is much more involved, but for both methods, it's a good idea to have some sort of map handy to show the actual office space and square footage measurements.

In Summary, Authors in business can benefit come tax time from understanding the complexities of Body and Setting, *ahem*, the Special Deductions available for Health Insurance and Home Office.

Chapter Nine
Supporting Characters

Employees
& Independent Contractors

In most novels, there are supporting characters—those who rally around the hero(ine) and help him/her along his/her way. The need for support also occurs in business, and building teams of "supporting characters" is a *MUST* for Authors.

There are basically two classifications of such characters: INDEPENDENT CONTRACTORS and EMPLOYEES. Differentiating between the two groups is very important, as the two are handled differently from a tax and legal standpoint.

Under Common Law Rules, anyone who performs services for you is generally your EMPLOYEE if you have the right to control *what* will be done and *how* it will be done. This is so even when you give an Employee freedom of action.

By contrast, the general rule to determine if an individual is an INDEPENDENT CONTRACTOR is if you, the person for whom the services are performed, have the right to control or direct *only the result* of the work and *not* the means and methods of accomplishing that result.

When determining whether the person providing services is an Employee or an Independent Contractor, all information that provides evidence of the degree of control and independence *MUST* be considered. Under Common Law Rules, there are twenty factors or elements used to determine the classification of a worker. Those twenty factors are often divided into THREE broad CATEGORIES with pertinent tests as follows:

1.) BEHAVIORAL—Does the company control or have the right to control what the worker does and how the worker does his or her job? An Employee is generally subject to the business's instructions about where, when, and how to work. The more detailed the instructions by the business, the more it points to a worker being an Employee versus an Independent Contractor.

> **"When determining whether the person providing services is an Employee or an Independent Contractor, all information that provides evidence of the degree of control and independence MUST be considered."**

2.) FINANCIAL—Are the business aspects of the worker's job controlled by the payer? These include things like how a worker is paid (by the hour or a flat fee), whether expenses are reimbursed and the great extent of those expenses, who provides supplies and equipment, if a worker's services are available to other companies in addition to your own, and if the worker is the one more at risk for a loss based on his/her investment in the services provided. Workers paid by the hour, reimbursed for all incidental expenses, and provided with the supplies required to accomplish their tasks typically fall in the Employee category, whereas workers paid a flat "project" fee and who handle their own incidental expenses and supply needs, and who might also offer their services to other companies are typically handled as Independent Contractors.

3.) TYPE OF RELATIONSHIP—Are there written contracts stating whether a worker is an Employee or Independent Contractor? Are Employee-type benefits offered (pension plan, insurance, vacation pay)? Will the relationship continue indefinitely rather than for a specific time or project? And is the work performed a key aspect of the business, which would give the employer the greater right to control and monitor the activities? The more the relationship between a business and worker points to one of ongoing service by the worker under the business's oversight, the more likely that worker is an Employee.

These three broad categories pose several basic questions for making a determination. The more clear and obvious the categories in which workers fall, the easier it is for a business owner to handle them correctly with regards to legal obligations and proper tax reporting.

So, why does classifying an individual correctly matter so much? What if you *don't* put workers in their proper category?

Well, the BIGGEST issues arise when a business classifies workers as Independent Contractors when they *should have* treated them as Employees. If you classify an Employee as an Independent Contractor and you have no reasonable basis for doing so, you may be held liable for all employment taxes for that worker, you may have to reimburse him/her for all business expenses they incurred while performing their job, you may be required to make payments under workers' compensation insurance based on their duties and pay, you would have to comply with all minimum wage and overtime laws, and you may have to provide the worker with benefits if he/she met the rules of any company benefit plans.

Sounds like a LOT, because it is!

Having Employees certainly means more accounting and tax handling/reporting versus using Independent Contractors. Employers must generally withhold Federal Income Taxes, withhold and match Social Security and Medicare Taxes, pay Unemployment Tax, and all pertinent State Taxes imposed on wages paid to an Employee. By contrast, a business does not withhold any taxes on payments to Independent Contractors. Using Independent Contractors also means that you/your company's legal liability for wrongful acts by an Independent Contractor is severely limited as compared to acts by an Employee because the relationship lacks the control, authority, and supervision found in an Employer-Employee relationship.

The advantages of hiring Independent Contractors are pretty clear, but again, *make sure* all workers you hire are classified correctly before automatically tossing them into that easier-to-manage group, or else risk a whole lot more complications and cost!

Okay, now that we are aware of *how* important it is to classify workers, let's move on to a typical supporting cast for Authors . . .

Generally, most Authors will hire freelancers who are classified as Independent Contractors. These include individuals *clearly* in business for themselves, offering expert services with which an Author has little skill and/or lack of time to handle on his/her own.

EXAMPLES of INDEPENDENT CONTRACTORS Authors (no matter how they are published) may hire:

- 📖 Web Site Designers
- 📖 Professional Editors
- 📖 CPAs
- 📖 Attorneys
- 📖 Marketing Professionals

Independently-Published Authors may ALSO hire:

- 📖 Professional Formatters
- 📖 Cover Designers
- 📖 Proofreaders
- 📖 Swag Designers
- 📖 Logo/Branding Professionals
- 📖 Book Trailer Creators

The earnings of any individual working as an Independent Contractor are commonly subject to Self-Employment Tax, but it is the responsibility of that Independent Contractor to handle paying their own taxes. However, Authors using Independent Contractors *will* need to acquire certain information for reporting purposes. A business owner's responsibility is to file a Form 1096 at year end to report to the IRS payments to Independent Contractors and to issue a Form 1099-MISC to each Independent Contractor that the business paid $600 or more to during the year. These Forms require having each Independent Contractor's contact information and Tax Identification Number, which can be acquired by having him/her fill out a Form W-9-Request for Taxpayer Identification and Certification. Attaining the

W-9 at time of service (or at least before you make payment) is best, as it ensures that you are prepared with the information needed at year end.

Additional notes:

_____

Note: Independent Contractors who are in business as Corporations (C-Corporations or S-Corporations) are exempt from receiving 1099s for services rendered.

_____

Note: businesses paying rent will also need to issue a 1099 for "Rents" paid equal to or in excess of $600 for the year.

Note: specific state(s) may have additional required filings.

Ready for EMPLOYEES?

Though many who provide services to Authors are Independent Contractors, I will mention TWO EXAMPLES of workers who could fall into the EMPLOYEE category:

1.) YOURSELF—Businesses structured as Corporations (or as an LLC using Corporation tax status) pay owners as Employees.

2.) PERSONAL ASSISTANT—I know Authors *(lucky ones!)* who pay personal assistants to accomplish a variety of tasks on a regular basis under the supervision and control of those Authors. These assistants are not performing their tasks in the same *independent* way a business owner/expert freelancer would, they are not licensed/insured/set up to manage clients, nor do they advertise themselves as a business often does. In short, they fall easily into the Employee classification.

Anytime a business has Employees, setting up and managing PAYROLL and its necessary functions is necessary. Before you run away at the mere mention of Payroll, allow me to at least familiarize you with the main rules and tasks involved. Basically, you would need to:

✓ Acquire a Federal Employer Identification Number (you cannot use your social security number for this). You will also need to check with your specific state(s) for State Employer Identification Number requirements.

✓ Have Employee(s) fill out a Form W-4-Employees Withholding Allowance Certificate and any State forms required. These are easily found online.

✓ Find out all of the pertinent Federal and State Withholding Taxes to be deducted from each paycheck. Applicable withholding tables can also be found online.

✓ Abide by and provide/display required Labor Law information (this basically lets Employees know their Federal and State Labor Rights).

✓ Determine the pay period used (weekly, bi-weekly, monthly, etc.).

✓ Provide Employees a paycheck with a check stub showing pertinent deductions (these can be in paper or digital format).

✓ Account for any sort of benefit and/or retirement plans implemented according to their rules.

✓ File Payroll Reports (most likely Quarterly) to the IRS and any pertinent States.

✓ Pay the IRS and pertinent States the Employee Withholdings and Employer-Imposed Taxes as they are due.

✓ File Annual Payroll Reports, including sending each Employee a year end W-2-Wage and Tax Statement.

✓ Handle any liens placed on an Employee's wages.

Handling Payroll can sound daunting, but it's really not that bad once you get the hang of it.

Okay, maybe some of you would rather poke a pen in your eye.

In that case, there are lots of Payroll service companies (including banks) or accounting firms who can handle this for you. Having employees can be really great and worth the extra effort. Do not let the extra tasks dissuade you. I mean, who doesn't want an awesome assistant or other "supporting character" at your beckon call?

No matter which group workers an Author hires fall into—Employees or Independent Contractors—these individuals are an important part of the success of an Author and his/her business. And managing legal and accounting tasks correctly is simply a part of the wheel of running any efficient business.

Chapter Ten
Flash Forward

Savings & Retirement

Now that we've gone over many of the *here and now* Bean-Counting topics, let us move on to the importance of thinking ahead, of *flashing forward* to those future years that await you.

Along with the freedom and control business ownership can yield, it also forces owners to be their own employers (figuratively or literally, depending on the business structure). Since the bulk of RETIREMENT SAVINGS is typically handled by an employer, business owners must then handle this type of savings for themselves.

The most basic and familiar type of retirement benefits is derived through payments into SOCIAL SECURITY—a system born from the Social Security Act of 1935, which provided for the "general welfare", including old age benefits for workers. The dollar amounts paid to fund this program are figured as a *percentage* of pay from workers, which is typically withheld from workers' paychecks and matched by their employers. Though pay taxed for Social Security purposes is most often pay from traditional payroll, in the case of Sole Proprietors and Partners, contributions are made to Social Security via the Self-Employment Tax computed on year-end personal tax filings. As explained in a previous chapter, Self Employment Tax takes care of both the employee and matching employer parts of Social Security

Tax. Basically, whether or not a business owner is paid via payroll (if his/her business is a Corporation) or with company net earnings (if his/her business is a Sole Proprietorship or Partnership), contributions are made into this mandatory fund.

Though Social Security is a required retirement program, it's important to understand that it does *not* act like a regular retirement account available to us in retirement. Yes, contributions are paid by individuals and their employers, and yes, those contributions are recorded, but *none* of the Social Security payments made are magically placed into *dedicated* savings accounts for those individuals. The system is not a direct savings system, but rather uses an individual's income and contributions over so many years to compute a *monthly entitlement* at retirement age. Dollars paid in *today* are actually supporting those retirees drawing benefits *today*. So, in 10, 20, 50 years retirees will draw from those future contributors.

Well, we can hope . . .

Why? Because the whole system is on increasingly shaky ground—some projections show that (unless some big changes are made) Social Security will be fully depleted by 2033, with the red zone starting in 2020. In addition, the age of receiving "full" benefits is being pushed up every year, and those elaborately-computed benefits are, well, *not* very elaborate. Those relying solely on Social Security benefits survive on extremely slim budgets.

So, what exactly is meant by the "full" age of retirement?

The actual age at which a retiree can begin to receive Social Security benefits is anywhere between age 62 and 70. Taking benefits early provides money for a longer period, but the monthly benefit amount will be less. Full retirement age—the age at which Social Security deems an individual eligible to receive his/her "full" benefit amount—is determined by a person's year of birth. Currently, for those born in the year 1960 and later, full retirement age is set at age 67. All things remaining the same, if a person in this category opted to receive benefits at age 62 instead of waiting until the full age of 67, his/her benefit amount would be reduced by 30% (35% for a spouse). Now, each person's financial situation will be different and each will dictate whether or not someone should take the reduced benefit early, wait until full retirement age, or wait all the way until age 70 for a higher benefit amount.

Note: benefit amounts do not increase beyond age 70.

You might wonder what these actual benefit amounts look like. Let's get down to some dollars and cents . . .

Benefit amounts are all quite variable, of course, with variances between individuals based on several factors, including annual income amounts for years worked, number of years worked where annual income met or exceeded minimum criteria, and whether or not full retirement age was reached before receiving benefits. But to provide an *idea* as to what actual benefits look like, according to the Social Security Administration:

"Average Monthly Benefits as of 01/15 were:

Retired worker: $1,328
Retired worker and aged spouse: 2,176
Disabled worker: 1,165
Disabled worker, spouse, and children: 1,976
Aged widow(er): 1,274
Widowed mother/father and 2 children: 2,680

Average Monthly benefit changes based on
the number of new entitlements as
well as the number of beneficia-
ries who come off of the
Social Security rolls
monthly."

I will add, again, that these averages are not only variable, but at risk of lowering without fixes to the program itself. But even if these numbers remained solid, they still reveal a minimal monthly living. Finding additional income sources to support ourselves in our sunset years is simply smart and necessary planning.

Now, there are those who have/will acquire wealth from other sources, including Authors who will earn sufficient royalties from their rocking chairs *(kudos!)*. But those lucky ducklings aside, many self-employed individuals will need to find OTHER TYPES OF RETIREMENT FUNDS in order to live beyond super skinny budgets. So, how does a small business owner achieve such a thing?

There are options . . .

Perhaps the easiest retirement savings to set up and fund is a TRADITIONAL IRA—Individual Retirement Arrangement or its often preferred cousin, the ROTH IRA. Both IRAs are personal savings vehicles available to most everyone, and each offers its own set of savings and tax advantages. There is no limit on how many IRA accounts (either sort) you own, so long as annual contributions stay within the annual allowable limits. The other nice thing about IRAs is that a non-working spouse can also own and contribute to them, so long as the other spouse has compensation and the couple files a joint tax return.

So, what are these limits I mentioned?

Contributions to all IRA accounts must not exceed your taxable income up to $5,500 ($6,500 if you are age 50 or older) in 2015. There are additional "phase-out" limits for those with high incomes when contributing to a ROTH IRA. For 2015, contribution limits for a ROTH IRA are applied when the "modified adjusted gross income" is equal to or exceeds $116,000 for single filers and $183,000 for married filing jointly filers. These phase-out limits do not apply to a Traditional IRA, however with this type of IRA, no regular contributions can be made once you reach the year that you turn 70 ½ years old.

On to some tax advantages . . .

Because the ROTH IRA is funded with *after-tax* dollars, it may have the best advantage with absolutely *zero* tax on withdrawals of contributions *and* all earnings *(woot-woot!)* once the account is over 5 years old (if less than 5 years old, penalties will be applied without a "special exception"). There are also no Required Distributions in retirement—basically, you can withdraw money as you see fit!

By comparison, the TRADITIONAL IRA is funded with *pre-tax* dollars (deferred income). This type of IRA allows for a tax deduction of contribution amounts in the year they are made, which can be a nice way to reduce your current tax bill. However, limits on tax deductible contributions may apply if you or your spouse has a retirement account through another employer and your Modified Adjusted Income (subtotal on your tax filing) exceeds $61,000 for a single filer or $98,000 for a married filing jointly filer (based on 2015 figures). Keep in mind that enjoying some tax savings now will mean that all later withdrawals of contributions *and* earnings will be subject to income tax. In addition, withdrawals are penalized if taken before age 59 ½ (unless funds are used for one of the "special exemption" items), and there are Required Minimum Distributions (RMDs) that must begin no later than age 70 ½. In fact, according to IRS:

> *"If an account owner fails to withdraw a RMD,*
> *fails to withdraw the full amount of the RMD,*
> *or fails to withdraw the RMD by the*
> *applicable deadline, the amount*
> *not withdrawn is taxed*
> *at 50%."*

Ouch!

Though I am partial to the ROTH IRA, a TRADITIONAL IRA is still a fine vessel for retirement savings with some tax advantages, as long as the owners make sure distributions are handled smartly. In fact, many individuals own *both* types of accounts to gain the advantages of both. In addition, rolling over, converting, or re-characterizing monies from one IRA type to the other has certain benefits. There are, of course, many rules with regards to moving money between such accounts, including some potentially lumpy tax consequences if things aren't handled wisely. But the bottom line is that an IRA, no matter the type, can provide some oh-so-nice additional monies for retirement.

IRAs are basically accounts set up and managed by *individuals*. There are also Retirement Accounts business owners can set up within their *businesses* to provide retirement funding for themselves and other employees (if any). Be aware that with any PLANS IMPLEMENTED BY A BUSINESS, there will be added costs (management, employer contributions for participating employees, etc.), but the ability for owners to substantially fund their own retirement accounts is a huge plus that can offset any burdens incurred by their businesses.

Larger companies will often implement what is known as a 401(k) PLAN, whereas smaller companies may choose to use either a SIMPLE IRA-Savings Investment Match Plan for Employees or a SEP IRA-Simplified Employee Pension.

Without going into too much detail, I will explain these accounts . . .

A 401(k) PLAN is more typically used by larger companies due to its complex rules, management costs, and reporting requirements, though a business of any size can set one up. In fact, if you are the *only* one working for your business, with no plan for hiring additional employees, owner-only Sole Proprietorships and partner-only Partnerships can set up what is known as a Solo 401(k) (specific and varying rules apply).

Basically, with 401(k) PLANS, employees *elect* to have portions of their income deferred—deducted from taxable income now and added later when withdrawn as distributions. Employers automatically deduct those employee contributions from paychecks before taxes are taken out and submit those contributions to the employee's 401(k) account. Employers can also contribute on an employee's behalf either through "matching" contributions of a certain percentage of salary/wages or at specified dollar amounts, so long as they keep within the annual limit rules. Matching is a phenomenal aspect of employer-hosted retirement accounts, as all employer-funded dollars increase the amount of savings for the employee (which is you in the case of an owner-employee), and employer contributions are typically deductible by the business.

There are several types of 401(k) PLANS, including Traditional 401(k) PLANS, SAFE HARBOR 401(k) PLANS, SIMPLE 401(k) PLANS, and as mentioned above, the SOLO 401(k) PLAN. Each type has its own set of rules and criteria requiring a full understanding, and all plans require an annual reporting via Form 5500 with the IRS.

Note: a Solo 401(k) does not currently require an annual filing if the fund is valued less than $250,000.

Some plans allow for employee contributions only, others provide for both employee and employer contributions, and others stipulate employer-only contributions. There are nondiscrimination tests required for many plans, which can be a tedious aspect of managing them. Whatever the plan, all 401(k) arrangements will require certain planning, administration, and ongoing tasks, which may/may not be something a business owner is either willing to tackle on his/her own or dole out to a professional account manager.

Perhaps the GREATEST reason a business owner would grab this plan by the horns is due to the annual contribution limits, which are *much* greater than those allowed for independently-managed TRADITIONAL and ROTH IRAs. For 2015, individuals aged 49 and under can contribute up to $18,000 per year (those 50 and over can contribute an additional $6,000) to a 401(k) PLAN. Employers can, if they choose to, match that $18,000 dollar for dollar *or* match an amount up to a certain percentage of the employee's annual income, *or* they can even opt to contribute more than the employee as long as the Total Annual Contributions from both employee and employer does not exceed the lesser of 100% of the employee's salary/wages or $53,000 (for 2015). This high allowance along with the variety of fund types often found within a 401(k) provides the potential for a nice accumulation of retirement dollars. In my opinion, it is a plan worthy of consideration. Even if it doesn't fit for your business now, it could very well find a place in your business down the road.

More commonly chosen by smaller companies is either a SIMPLE IRA or SEP IRA, as both plans are typically easier to set up and manage as compared to the 401(k). Neither of them requires annual plan filings, and they both allow for Annual Contributions that are higher than TRADITIONAL and ROTH IRAs, making them appealing options for business owners trying to save for the future.

Some CLARIFICATION AND DIFFERENCES between these two plans include:

❖ The SIMPLE IRA is set up for small businesses, generally with fewer than 100 employees. The SEP IRA is available to any sized business (though, again, more popular with small businesses).

❖ The SIMPLE IRA must be the *only* retirement plan provided by the employer. No such restriction with a SEP PLAN.

❖ The SIMPLE IRA is funded by employee contributions (deferred income) and/or required employer contributions that *either* match an employee's contribution up to 3% of his/her total wages *or* that are a 2% non-elective contribution for eligible employees. By contrast, a SEP IRA is funded *only* by the employer, and the employer *must* contribute the same percentage of compensation to employee accounts as he/she contributes to his/her own.

❖ For 2015, the SIMPLE IRA has Annual Employee Contribution limits of $12,500 ($15,500 for those aged 50 and over), not including what is also employer-matched. Contributions an employer can make to an employee's SEP IRA cannot exceed the lesser of 25% of the employee's compensation or $53,000.

Note: for Sole Proprietors not on payroll, compensation is figured in a computation using net profits and self-employment tax, and certain limits apply.

SIMPLE IRAs and SEP IRAs both follow similar rules with TRADITIONAL IRAs when it comes to distributions: Distributions taken in retirement are taxed in the year they are taken; distributions taken before age 59 ½ may be subject to an additional penalty tax if certain hardship exemptions do not apply (additional penalties are placed on distributions taken from a SIMPLE IRA within the first two years of participation); and as with TRADITIONAL IRAs, individuals must take Required Minimum Distributions (RMDs) once they are over 70 ½.

In addition to all of the retirement options I have described thus far, there are many OTHER WAYS an individual and/or business owner can accumulate funds for retirement. Several types of annuities, stock funds, bonds, real estate investments, bank CDs, and even whole or universal life insurance policies with cash savings features can offer additional ways to save. Keep in mind that pretty much *all* methods of saving for retirement take time, especially when it comes to having your investments work for you (earning equity in real estate, dividends on stocks, interest on CDs, etc.). I encourage everyone, especially those depending solely on themselves for retirement income, to dedicate some effort into exploring all of the options and planning for those sunset years.

A good rule of thumb: Invest between 10-15% of your annual gross income into retirement savings *and* start doing this as early as possible! Retirement should be about relaxing and enjoying the remainder of our lives, not about scraping for dollars and cents.

Afterword

I have briefly explained numerous areas of accounting and taxation for small business owners, particularly Authors in business. Though this guide is by no means meant to be the sole resource used, I do believe the information provided gives plenty of "food" to churn in the minds of those serious about running a professional business.

Here is a handy recap CHECKLIST:

- ✓ Determine if your endeavor is a Business or Hobby
- ✓ Choose and implement an Entity Structure for your Business
- ✓ Set up and Keep Books properly
- ✓ Set up and manage Sales and Use Tax when and where required
- ✓ Understand the different Business Taxes
- ✓ Recognize, track, and budget for Common Expenses
- ✓ Recognize, track, and budget for Complex Expenses
- ✓ Become clear about Employees versus Independent Contractors, and handle each accordingly
- ✓ Plan and save for Retirement

And one last thought on ATTITUDE . . .

Obviously, being thrifty in our spending and saving in tax dollars is a goal many of us have, but keep in mind that, *generally speaking*, paying bills and taxes is also a good thing. Why? Because there is much to be grateful for when we *have* the means to pay for things and when we *earn enough* to generate taxes. Show your money respect and it will respect you right back. Become a mini Bean Counter (or at least *pay attention* to the information a reputable Bean Counter provides you), appreciate *every* dollar received, show gratitude for *every* dollar spent on necessary and desirous purchases, and watch how things shift for the better.

Gratitude is a powerful thing—sort of like *Energy Currency*—and yes, that might sound *woo-woo*, but the beliefs of this oddly ambidextrous Author-Accountant include the notion that a positive attitude about money helps to nurture a positive flow of it in our lives.

Okay, now it's time to get counting!

Resources

The good old IRS site provides detailed rules on Federal taxation:
https://www.irs.gov/

The QuickBooks site offers instruction on using QuickBooks software and articles on business and bookkeeping tips:
http://quickbooks.intuit.com/

The Turbo Tax site has a handy "Tools and Tips" tab with helpful information:
https://turbotax.intuit.com/

EFTPS: The Electronic Federal Tax Payment System is a free site provided by the U.S. Department of the Treasury:
https://www.eftps.gov/eftps/

The official Federal Social Security site:
https://www.ssa.gov/retire/

Investopedia offers a variety of articles on multiple financial topics:
http://www.investopedia.com/

The Sales Tax Institute offers courses and training in sales tax and has a "Resources" tab with helpful information:
http://www.salestaxinstitute.com

NOLO LAW for ALL is a helpful legal resource, which posts many articles on taxation:
http://www.nolo.com/

Indie-Visible provides a resourceful PubHub for writers, including the series from which this book originated:
http://www.indie-visible.com

Glossary

Short List of Terms

Assets—items a company owns and uses to operate the company.

Balance Sheet—financial statement that tracks assets, liabilities, and owner's (or shareholder's) equity.

C Corporation—an independent legal entity owned by shareholders.

Capital Expenses— expenses derived from the purchase of depreciable assets.

Cost of Goods Sold (COGS)—an amount computed using a formula that takes Inventory and Costs of Sales into consideration.

Depreciation—an income tax deduction that allows a taxpayer to recover the cost or other basis of certain property; an annual allowance for the wear and tear, deterioration, or obsolescence of property.

Double Entry Bookkeeping—method where at least two entries are recorded for every financial transaction in order to create balanced journal entries.

Employee—anyone who performs services for a business, and who the business has the right to control regarding what job duties will be done and how they will be done.

Equity—overall investment in a company.

Estimated Tax—estimated amount of tax on income that is not subject to withholding; the method used to pay in enough taxes before an annual tax return is filed.

Financial Statements—standard accounting reports used for a variety of business purposes, including the completion of required tax filings.

General Partnership—an entity where all partners are engaged in the operations of the partnership.

Independent Contractor—one who acts as an independent business owner; one who provides a service to others while retaining the right over the means and methods of accomplishing that service.

Journal Entry—a balanced bookkeeping entry used to record a financial transaction made by a business.

Liabilities—a company's financial obligations

Limited Liability Company (LLC)—a hybrid entity structure allowed by state statute.

Nexus—term used for a business that has a sufficient physical presence in a particular state through the permanent or temporary presence of people or of property.

Partnership—an entity that allows the presence of multiple owners, each contributing to the business capital and each sharing in the profits and losses; can be either a General or Limited Partnership.

Profit and Loss Statement—a financial statement that shows a summary of the revenues, costs, and expenses for a period of time.

S Corporation—an independent legal entity owned by a maximum of 100 shareholders.

Schedule C-Profit or Loss From Business for a Sole Proprietor—form used by taxpayers who are independent contractors or sole owners of a business to report income or loss from their business activities.

Self-Employment Tax—a Social Security and Medicare tax primarily for individuals who work for themselves.

Single Entry Bookkeeping—method where a single entry is used to record each financial transaction; used only with cash-basis accounting.

Sole Proprietorship—an unincorporated business with no existence or legal distinction separate and apart from its owner.

Statement of Cash Flows—a financial statement that shows the actual cash flow of a business.

About
the Author

Once-upon-a-time, **Christina Mercer** worked as a CPA. Though she retired that formal hat, you can still find numbers buzzing around her head. She is also an award-winning author of fiction for children and young adults. She currently resides in Northern California enjoying life with her husband, sons, a pack of large dogs, and about 100,000 honeybees.

www.christinamercer.com

www.ingramcontent.com/pod-product-compliance
Lightning Source LLC
Chambersburg PA
CBHW060046210326
41520CB00009B/1286